1001 ESSENTIAL VOCABULARY WORDS
FOR ELEMENTARY ENGLISH LEARNERS

CEDU 쎄듀는 A **C**omprehensive **E**nglish e**DU**cation(종합적 영어교육)의 약자입니다.

초등코치 천일문 시리즈
with 세이펜

원어민 음성을 실시간 반복학습	녹음 기능으로 쉐도잉 발음교정	게임 기능으로 재미있고 유익하게

초등코치 천일문 시리즈 Sentence 1권~5권, Grammar 1권~3권, Voca&Story 1권~2권 모두
세이펜을 활용하여 원어민 MP3 음성 재생 서비스를 이용할 수 있습니다.
(책 앞면 하단에 세이펜 로고 SAYPEN🔲가 있습니다.)

세이펜 핀파일 다운로드 안내

STEP ① 세이펜과 컴퓨터를 USB 케이블로 연결하세요.

STEP ② 쎄듀북 홈페이지(www.cedubook.com)에 접속 후, 학습자료실 메뉴에서 학습할 교재를 찾아 이동합니다.

> 초·중등교재 ▶ 어휘 ▶ 학습교재 클릭 ▶ 세이펜 핀파일 자료 클릭
> ▶ 다운로드 (저장을 '다른 이름으로 저장'으로 변경하여 저장소를 USB로 변경) ▶ 완료

STEP ③ 음원 다운로드가 완료되면 세이펜과 컴퓨터의 USB 케이블을 분리하세요.

STEP ④ 세이펜을 분리하면 "시스템을 초기화 중입니다. 잠시만 기다려 주세요" 라는 멘트가 나옵니다.

STEP ⑤ 멘트 종료 후 세이펜을 〈초등코치 천일문 Voca&Story〉 표지의 제목 부분에 대보세요.
효과음이 나온 후 바로 학습을 시작할 수 있습니다.

참고사항

◆ 세이펜에서 제작된 모든 기종(기존에 보유하고 계신 기종도 호환 가능)으로 사용이 가능합니다.

　단, Sentence 교재의 Role-Play 기능은 레인보우 SBS-1000 기종에서만 구동됩니다. (신규 구매자는 SBS-1000 이후 모델의 구매를 권장합니다.)

◆ 모든 기종은 세이펜에서 권장하는 최신 펌웨어 업데이트를 진행해 주시기 바랍니다. 업데이트는 세이펜 홈페이지(www.saypen.com)에서 가능합니다.

◆ 초등코치 천일문 시리즈의 핀파일은 쎄듀북 홈페이지(www.cedubook.com)와 세이펜 홈페이지(www.saypen.com)에서 모두 다운로드 가능합니다.

◆ 세이펜을 이용하지 않는 학습자는 쎄듀북 홈페이지 부가학습자료, 교재 내 QR코드 이미지 등을 활용하여 원어민 음성으로 학습하실 수 있습니다.

◆ 기타 문의사항은 www.cedubook.com / 02-3272-4766으로 연락 바랍니다.

초등코치

천일문
voca&story

✦ ✦ ✦

2

저자

김기훈 現 ㈜ 쎄듀 대표이사
現 메가스터디 영어영역 대표강사
前 서울특별시 교육청 외국어 교육정책자문위원회 위원

저서 천일문 〈입문편 · 기본편 · 핵심편 · 완성편〉 / 초등코치 천일문 / 천일문 Grammar
첫단추 BASIC / 쎄듀 본영어 / 어휘끝 / 어법끝 / 문법의 골든룰 101
절대평가 PLAN A / 리딩 플랫폼 / 거침없이 Writing / Reading Relay
독해가 된다 시리즈 / The 리딩플레이어 / 빈칸백서 / 오답백서
첫단추 Button Up / 파워업 Power Up / ALL씀 서술형 시리즈
수능영어 절대유형 / 수능실감 등

쎄듀 영어교육연구센터
쎄듀 영어교육센터는 영어 컨텐츠에 대한 전문지식과 경험을 바탕으로
최고의 교육 컨텐츠를 만들고자 최선의 노력을 다하는 전문가 집단입니다.

인지영 선임연구원 **· 장혜승** 주임연구원

마케팅	콘텐츠 마케팅 사업본부
영업	문병구
제작	정승호
인디자인 편집	로즈앤북스
표지 디자인	윤혜영, 이연수
내지 디자인	에피그램
영문교열	Eric Scheusner

Foreword

〈초등코치 천일문 Voca & Story〉 시리즈를 펴내며

초등 영단어, 어떻게 시작해야 할까요?

영어를 배울 때, 대부분 가장 먼저 알파벳을 익힌 후 파닉스, 그리고 단어의 순서로 자연스럽게 학습하게 됩니다. 단어는 초등학교에서 배우는 의사소통 표현의 바탕이 되고 나아가 중학교에서 익히게 될 문법과 독해의 기초가 됩니다. 따라서 단어를 얼마나 알고 있는지가 영어 학습에 투자해야 하는 시간을 좌우합니다.

학습한 내용을 빠르게 흡수하고, 들리는 대로 따라 말할 수 있는 초등학생 시기가 영단어 기본기를 쌓기에 가장 적절할 때입니다. 눈으로 보고 귀로 듣고 입으로 먼저 학습하는 습관을 기를 수 있기 때문이지요.

〈초등코치 천일문 Voca & Story〉 시리즈는 초등학생이 꼭 알아야 하는 단어를 엄선하여 수록하였습니다. **교육부 권장 초등 어휘 800개와 그밖에 초등 필수 어휘까지 총 1,001개의 어휘와 짧은 스토리 예문으로 구성되었습니다.**

| 단어의 쓰임까지 학습해야 진정한 단어 학습입니다.

단어의 뜻만으로는 그 쓰임을 정확하게 파악하기 어렵습니다. 주어진 상황에 따른 단어의 쓰임과 변화형, 즉 단어 응용력을 기르는 것도 중요합니다. 〈초등코치 천일문 Voca & Story〉는 학습자들이 정확하게 단어의 의미를 이해할 수 있도록 앞뒤 상황이 제시된 짧은 스토리 예문들을 삽화를 곁들여 재미있게 구성하였습니다.

| 암기 효과를 높인 효율적인 학습이 되도록 설계했습니다.

'단어-뜻' 단순 암기가 아닌 듣기, 말하기, 쓰기, 읽기의 다양한 활동으로 쉽고 빠르게 단어를 암기할 수 있습니다. 이러한 학습법은 기계적인 암기법보다 암기 효과를 오랫동안 지속시키는 데 중요한 역할을 합니다.

짧은 스토리들을 통해 쌓은 영단어 기본기와 올바른 단어 학습법은 앞으로의 영어 학습에 있어 자신감의 바탕이 될 것입니다. 〈초등코치 Voca & Story〉 시리즈와의 만남을 통해 보다 쉽고 즐거운 영단어 학습을 경험하기를 희망합니다.

저 자

Preview

QR코드
휴대폰을 통해 QR코드를 인식하면, 본문의 모든 단어, 스토리의 MP3 파일이 재생됩니다.

🖊 세이펜을 대면 전체 단어를 두 번씩 들을 수 있습니다.

🖊 각 단어에 대면 원어민의 발음을 들을 수 있습니다.

🖊 녹음 기능을 통해 단어를 직접 녹음해 볼 수 있습니다.

🖊 자신이 녹음한 발음을 들을 수 있습니다.

🖊 각 단어에 대면 원어민의 발음과 우리말 뜻을 들을 수 있습니다.

🖊 각 단어에 대면 원어민의 발음을 들을 수 있습니다.

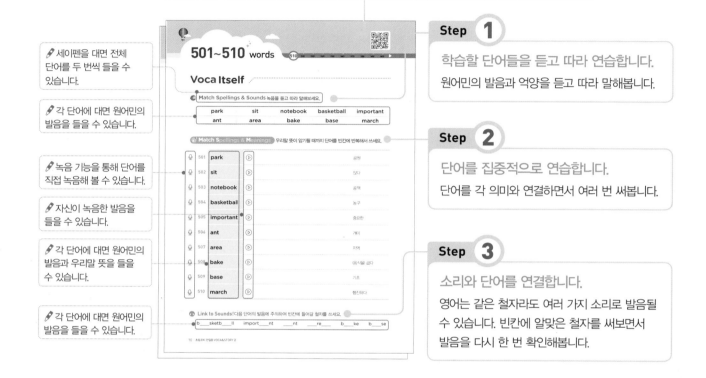

Step 1

학습할 단어들을 듣고 따라 연습합니다.
원어민의 발음과 억양을 듣고 따라 말해봅니다.

Step 2

단어를 집중적으로 연습합니다.
단어를 각 의미와 연결하면서 여러 번 써봅니다.

Step 3

소리와 단어를 연결합니다.
영어는 같은 철자라도 여러 가지 소리로 발음될 수 있습니다. 빈칸에 알맞은 철자를 써보면서 발음을 다시 한 번 확인해봅니다.

Step 4

단어의 달라지는 형태와 의미를 확인합니다.
동사가 문장에서 쓰일 때 형태나 의미가 어떻게 바뀌는지 볼 수 있습니다.

Step 5

빈칸에 알맞은 단어를 채워 스토리를 완성합니다.
재미있는 스토리로 단어의 쓰임을 학습할 수 있습니다. '단어-뜻'만 연결해서 암기하는 것보다 더 효과적으로 학습 내용을 오래 기억할 수 있습니다.

🖊 각 번호에 대면 해당 번호의 스토리 전체 내용을 들을 수 있습니다.

🖊 각 문장에 대면 원어민의 정확한 발음과 억양을 들을 수 있습니다.

*번역 기능 | 원어민 음성을 들은 후, T 버튼을 짧게 누르면 해석 음원을 들을 수 있습니다.

Step 6

Review를 통해 50개 단어씩 확인 학습합니다.

🖊 시작 버튼 (ON)에 대면 퀴즈를 시작할 수 있습니다. 종료 시에는 종료 버튼 (OFF)를 누릅니다.

🖊 재생 버튼 (▷)에 대면 10개 단어가 랜덤으로 재생됩니다.

🖊 재생되는 각 단어의 우리말 뜻에 세이펜을 대면 정답음이 나옵니다.
*세 번 틀리면 다음 문제로 넘어갑니다.

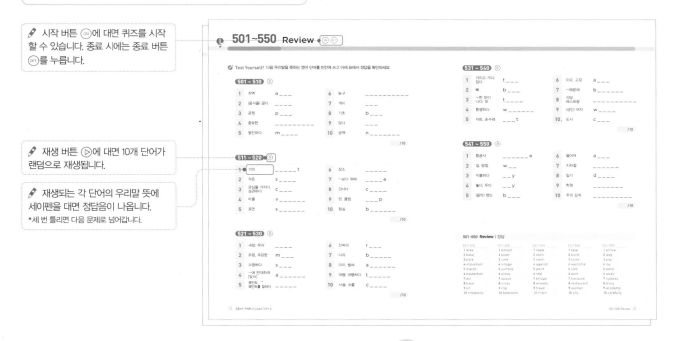

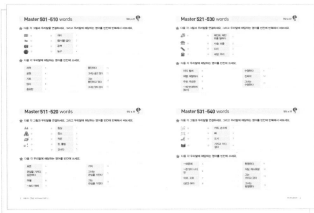

Step 7

워크북으로 배운 단어들을 복습합니다.

부가서비스 활용하기 쎄듀북 홈페이지(www.cedubook.com)에서 MP3 파일과 어휘자동출제 프로그램을 다운로드받으실 수 있습니다.

〈초등코치 천일문 Voca & Story〉 부가서비스 자료에는 본문의 모든 단어와 스토리의 MP3 파일 그리고 어휘자동출제 프로그램이 들어있습니다.

- **MP3 파일** 원어민 성우의 생생하고 정확한 발음과 억양을 확인할 수 있습니다.
  단어는 2회씩 녹음 되어있습니다.

- **어휘자동출제 프로그램** 교재에 실린 단어들을 사용하여 단어 시험지를 생성해줍니다. 출제 범위와 문제 유형을 선택할 수 있습니다.
  프로그램을 통해서 더욱 손쉽게 만들어진 단어 시험지로 완벽하게 복습할 수 있습니다.

세이펜 활용하기 〈초등코치 천일문 Voca & Story〉는 세이펜이 적용된 도서입니다. 세이펜을 영어에 가져다 대기만 하면 원어민이 들려주는 생생한 영어 발음과 억양을 바로 확인할 수 있습니다.

Contents 📖

권두부록 **주제별 단어** ─ 묶어서 공부하면 더 쉬운 단어들!

책속책 **WORKBOOK** | 정답과 해설

Study Plan

<초등코치 천일문 Voca & Story 2> 학습 계획표

★ 30일 완성!

1일차	501~520 words, 워크북
2일차	521~540 words, 워크북
3일차	541~550 words, 워크북 / Review 501~550
4일차	551~570 words, 워크북
5일차	571~590 words, 워크북
6일차	591~600 words, 워크북 / Review 551~600
7일차	601~620 words, 워크북
8일차	621~640 words, 워크북
9일차	641~650 words, 워크북 / Review 601~650
10일차	651~670 words, 워크북
11일차	671~690 words, 워크북
12일차	691~700 words, 워크북 / Review 651~700
13일차	701~720 words, 워크북
14일차	721~740 words, 워크북
15일차	741~750 words, 워크북 / Review 701~750
16일차	751~770 words, 워크북
17일차	771~790 words, 워크북
18일차	791~800 words, 워크북 / Review 751~800
19일차	801~820 words, 워크북
20일차	821~840 words, 워크북
21일차	841~850 words, 워크북 / Review 801~850
22일차	851~870 words, 워크북
23일차	871~890 words, 워크북
24일차	891~900 words, 워크북 / Review 851~900
25일차	901~920 words, 워크북
26일차	921~940 words, 워크북
27일차	941~950 words, 워크북 / Review 901~950
28일차	951~970 words, 워크북
29일차	971~990 words, 워크북
30일차	991~1001 words, 워크북 / Review 951~1001

★ 20일 완성!

1일차	501~530 words, 워크북
2일차	531~550 words, 워크북 / Review 501~550
3일차	551~580 words, 워크북
4일차	581~600 words, 워크북 / Review 551~600
5일차	601~630 words, 워크북
6일차	631~650 words, 워크북 / Review 601~650
7일차	651~680 words, 워크북
8일차	681~700 words, 워크북 / Review 651~700
9일차	701~730 words, 워크북
10일차	731~750 words, 워크북 / Review 701~750
11일차	751~780 words, 워크북
12일차	781~800 words, 워크북 / Review 751~800
13일차	801~830 words, 워크북
14일차	831~850 words, 워크북 / Review 801~850
15일차	851~880 words, 워크북
16일차	881~900 words, 워크북 / Review 851~900
17일차	901~930 words, 워크북
18일차	931~950 words, 워크북 / Review 901~950
19일차	951~980 words, 워크북
20일차	981~1001 words, 워크북 / Review 951~1001

Family 가족

- grandparents 조부모 ((외)할아버지, (외)할머니)
- grandfather 할아버지, 외할아버지 (=grandpa)
- grandmother 할머니, 외할머니 (=grandma)
- parents 부모
- father 아버지
- dad 아빠 (=daddy)
- mother 어머니
- mom 엄마 (=mommy)
- brother 남동생, 오빠, 형
- sister 여동생, 언니, 누나
- son 아들
- daughter 딸

호칭

- Mr. ~씨 (남자의 성이나 이름 앞에)
  e.g. Mr. Kim, Mr. Brown
- Ms. ~씨 (여자의 성이나 이름 앞에)
- Miss ~양, ~씨 (결혼하지 않은 여성)
- Mrs. ~ 부인 (결혼한 여성)
- sir 님, 귀하, 선생
  e.g. Excuse me, sir. (실례합니다.)

대명사 (명사를 대신하는 말)

- I 나
- you 너
- he 그
- she 그녀
- we 우리
- they 그들
- it 그것
- this 이것
- these 이것들
- that 저것
- those 저것들

Face 얼굴

- eye 눈
- nose 코
- ear 귀
- mouth 입
- lip 입술
- tooth(teeth) 이, 치아

Body 몸, 신체

- head 머리
- hair 털, 머리털
- neck 목
- shoulder 어깨
- arm 팔
- hand 손
- finger 손가락
- leg 다리
- foot(feet) 발
- toe 발가락

Color 색깔

- black 검은색
- blue 파란색
- brown 갈색
- gold 금색
- green 녹색, 초록색
- gray/grey 회색
- pink 분홍색
- red 빨간색
- white 흰색
- yellow 노란색

Fruit 과일

- apple 사과
- banana 바나나
- grape 포도
- lemon 레몬
- orange 오렌지
- kiwi 키위
- pear 배
- strawberry 딸기
- watermelon 수박

Voca Itself

🔊 **Match Spellings & Sounds** 녹음을 듣고 따라 말해보세요.

park	sit	notebook	basketball	important
ant	area	bake	base	march

Match Spellings & Meanings 우리말 뜻이 암기될 때까지 단어를 빈칸에 반복해서 쓰세요.

🎤 501	**park**	▷		공원
🎤 502	**sit**	▷		앉다
🎤 503	**notebook**	▷		공책
🎤 504	**basketball**	▷		농구
🎤 505	**important**	▷		중요한
🎤 506	**ant**	▷		개미
🎤 507	**area**	▷		지역
🎤 508	**bake**	▷		(음식을) 굽다
🎤 509	**base**	▷		기초
🎤 510	**march**	▷		행진하다

🔊 **Link to Sounds!** 다음 단어의 발음에 주의하여 빈칸에 들어갈 철자를 쓰세요.

b____sketb____ll   import____nt   ____nt   ____re____   b____ke   b____se

Voca in Stories

정답과 해설 p.2

⭐ 몇몇 단어들은 문장에서 쓰일 때 형태나 의미가 조금 바뀌기도 해요.

502 • She is **sit**ting 그녀는 앉아 있다   510 • He is **march**ing 그는 행진하고 있다
508 • She is **bak**ing 그녀는 굽고 있다

Fill in the Blanks 다음 글을 읽고 빈칸에 가장 알맞은 단어를 넣어 보세요.

1 I am new in this _____. Where is the nearest library in this town?

2 We are at a festival.
축제
The band is _____ now.
It looks great!

3 Reading and writing is the _____ of learning. They are very important in all subjects.

4 A boy is sitting on the ground. He is watching an _____. The _____ is carrying some food.

5 Mom is _____ some chocolate chip cookies now. They are my favorite!

6 Many people run and ride bikes in the _____. It is a nice place to exercise.

7  The kids are playing _____. "Shoot the ball
숫을 하다
now!" But, the boy missed.
It didn't go into the basket.

8 At the beginning of the school year, I always buy new _____s. It feels like a new start.

9 Exercise every day!
It's _____
for your health.
You will feel better, too.

10 Jenny is _____ in a chair. What is she doing? Is she reading a book? No, she is sleeping now.

Voca Itself

🎧 **Match Spellings & Sounds** 녹음을 듣고 따라 말해보세요.

care	place	cross	almost	above
bedroom	clip	small	surface	village

Match Spellings & Meanings 우리말 뜻이 암기될 때까지 단어를 빈칸에 반복해서 쓰세요.

🎤 511	**care**	▷	관심을 가지다, 상관하다
🎤 512	**place**	▷	장소
🎤 513	**cross**	▷	건너다
🎤 514	**almost**	▷	거의
🎤 515	**above**	▷	~보다 위에
🎤 516	**bedroom**	▷	침실
🎤 517	**clip**	▷	핀, 클립
🎤 518	**small**	▷	작은
🎤 519	**surface**	▷	표면
🎤 520	**village**	▷	마을

🎧 **Link to Sounds!** 다음 단어의 발음에 주의하여 빈칸에 들어갈 철자를 쓰세요.

c____re   ____lmost   ____bove   sm____ll   vill____ge

Voca in Stories

⭐ 몇몇 단어들은 문장에서 쓰일 때 형태나 의미가 조금 바뀌기도 해요.

511 • She **care**s 그녀는 관심을 가진다
 • He **care**d 그는 관심을 가졌다

Fill in the Blanks 다음 글을 읽고 빈칸에 가장 알맞은 단어를 넣어 보세요.

1 Dan lives in a small _____ . It is in the countryside. In his free time, he likes to walk. He enjoys nature.

2 It is 2:55. School finishes at 3 o'clock. It is _____ time to go home.

3 Jane has pieces of paper. She needs to hold them together. "Do you have any paper _____ s?"

4  Tim's family moved to a new house. It has four _____ s and two bathrooms.

5 My sweater is too _____ for me now. I need a bigger one. Maybe I should ask my mother.

6 When you _____ the street, look both ways. _____ the street when all the cars stop.

7 Tom is on the plane now. He is looking out the window. He sees beautiful clouds under the plane. It is flying _____ the clouds.

8 This mall has many shops. They have sales all the time. Everyone loves this _____ .

9 My parents _____ about me. They always listen to me and give advice.

10 The _____ of the ice is very smooth at the ice
매끄러운   스케이트장
rink today. Many kids enjoy skating there.

Voca Itself

🎧 **Match Spellings & Sounds** 녹음을 듣고 따라 말해보세요.

swim	travel	real	already	against
bridge	cage	chain	main	paint

Match Spellings & Meanings 우리말 뜻이 암기될 때까지 단어를 빈칸에 반복해서 쓰세요.

🎤 521	**swim**	▷		수영하다
🎤 522	**travel**	▷		여행; 여행하다
🎤 523	**real**	▷		진짜의
🎤 524	**already**	▷		이미, 벌써
🎤 525	**against**	▷		～에 반대하여[맞서]
🎤 526	**bridge**	▷		다리
🎤 527	**cage**	▷		새장; 우리
🎤 528	**chain**	▷		사슬, 쇠줄
🎤 529	**main**	▷		주된, 주요한
🎤 530	**paint**	▷		페인트; 페인트를 칠하다

🔊 **Link to Sounds!** 다음 단어의 발음에 주의하여 빈칸에 들어갈 철자를 쓰세요.

ag_____nst   ch___n   m___n   p___nt

Voca in Stories

⭐ 몇몇 단어들은 문장에서 쓰일 때 형태나 의미가 조금 바뀌기도 해요.

521 • She **swims** 그녀는 수영한다

Fill in the Blanks 다음 글을 읽고 빈칸에 가장 알맞은 단어를 넣어 보세요.

1
The red team and the blue team are playing _____ each other.
서로
Which team will win?

2
My town will have a festival. The _____ event will be fireworks!
불꽃놀이

3
"Teacher, I finished the test," Jane said. The teacher was very surprised. "_____? You have more time, Jane," said the teacher.

4

The children have blue _____.
The walls of the room were white before. Soon, they will be blue.

5
There is a new _____ now.
So, people can cross the river by car. They don't need a boat.

6
"Is this yours? There is a diamond in it. Is it _____?" Jane asked. "Please don't touch anything," said Jane's sister.

7

Mike lost two bikes last year. So, this year he bought a new _____ and lock.
자물쇠

8
Kate has two pet birds. But the _____ looks too small for them. They need a new house.

9
I want to _____ to many countries.
I want to meet new people and learn new things.

10
Jenny likes to _____.
Every summer she goes to the pool and _____ there.

Voca Itself

🎙 **Match Spellings & Sounds** 녹음을 듣고 따라 말해보세요.

aunt	because	bone	cart	city
restaurant	take	taste	welcome	woman

Match Spellings & Meanings 우리말 뜻이 암기될 때까지 단어를 빈칸에 반복해서 쓰세요.

🎙	531	**aunt**	▷	이모, 고모
🎙	532	**because**	▷	~때문에
🎙	533	**bone**	▷	뼈
🎙	534	**cart**	▷	카트, 손수레
🎙	535	**city**	▷	도시
🎙	536	**restaurant**	▷	식당, 레스토랑
🎙	537	**take**	▷	가지고 가다; 잡다
🎙	538	**taste**	▷	~한 맛이 나다; 맛
🎙	539	**welcome**	▷	환영하다
🎙	540	**woman**	▷	(성인) 여자

🔊 **Link to Sounds!** 다음 단어의 발음에 주의하여 빈칸에 들어갈 철자를 쓰세요.

_____nt   bec_____se   rest_____rant

Voca in Stories

⭐ 몇몇 단어들은 문장에서 쓰일 때 형태나 의미가 조금 바뀌기도 해요.

537 • He **took** 그는 가지고 갔다   539 • She **welcomed** 그녀는 환영했다

Fill in the Blanks 다음 글을 읽고 빈칸에 가장 알맞은 단어를 넣어 보세요.

1 We are going out for dinner. "Do you like pasta? There is a great _____ near here," says my dad.

2 I love watermelons 수박 because they _____ very sweet.

3 Seoul is a big _____. You can see many tall buildings, and a lot of cars and buses here.

4 When my _____ visits us, she tells funny stories about my dad. "When your dad was little, he cried a lot," she said.

5  My dog Oliver plays with _____s every day. He likes to chew on them. 씹다

6 "Why does Lucy look so happy today?" Lucy's dad asked. "She is excited _____ it is Christmas tomorrow," said her mom.

7 Mike cannot find his umbrella. "Who _____ my umbrella? Mom? Dad? Jane?"

8  Jane and her mom were at a supermarket. She pushed a _____ for her mom.

9 "Do you know that _____ over there?" Sara asked. "She is my new English teacher."

10 Tom visited his grandmother last weekend. She _____ him with a warm smile.

Voca Itself

🔵 **Match Spellings & Sounds** 녹음을 듣고 따라 말해보세요.

way	academy	airline	away	band
carefully	diary	lay	pay	subway

Match Spellings & Meanings 우리말 뜻이 암기될 때까지 단어를 빈칸에 반복해서 쓰세요.

🎤 541	way	▷		길, 방법
🎤 542	academy	▷		학원
🎤 543	airline	▷		항공사
🎤 544	away	▷		떨어져
🎤 545	band	▷		(음악) 밴드
🎤 546	carefully	▷		주의 깊게
🎤 547	diary	▷		일기
🎤 548	lay	▷		놓다, 두다
🎤 549	pay	▷		지불하다
🎤 550	subway	▷		지하철

🎧 **Link to Sounds!** 다음 단어의 발음에 주의하여 빈칸에 들어갈 철자를 쓰세요.

w____   aw____   l____   p____   subw____

Voca in Stories

⭐ 몇몇 단어들은 문장에서 쓰일 때 형태나 의미가 조금 바뀌기도 해요.

548 •She laid 그녀는 **놓았다**　　　　549 •He paid 그는 **지불했다**

✏ Fill in the Blanks 다음 글을 읽고 빈칸에 가장 알맞은 단어를 넣어 보세요.

1 Tom draws really well. He studies drawing at an art _____.

2 Amy's best friend lives far _____ from here. She moved to another country.

3 Mary's family had dinner at a restaurant. Her dad went to the cashier. He _____ for the food.
종업원

4 Diana and John are walking home together. "I am going this _____. What about you?" said John.

5 Tom's father goes to work by _____. He leaves his car at home. He doesn't like traffic.
교통량

6 I write everything in my _____. So, I don't like it when people try to open and read my _____.

7 My brother wants to become an _____ pilot. Pilots can travel all around the world!
조종사

8 Jake played the guitar in his school _____. But he moved to another city. The _____ will miss him.

9 Lucy's mother got a new car. She is not a good driver yet. So, she drives very _____.

10 "The test is over," the teacher said. Sara _____ her pencil on her desk.

501~550 Review (ON) (OFF)

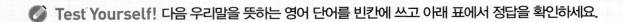

✏️ **Test Yourself!** 다음 우리말을 뜻하는 영어 단어를 빈칸에 쓰고 아래 표에서 정답을 확인하세요.

▶ 501 ~ 510

1	지역	a _ _ _	6	농구	_ _ _ _ _ _ _ _ _ _
2	(음식을) 굽다	_ _ _ _	7	개미	_ _ _
3	공원	p _ _ _	8	기초	b _ _ _
4	중요한	_ _ _ _ _ _ _ _ _	9	앉다	_ _ _
5	행진하다	m _ _ _ _	10	공책	n _ _ _ _ _ _ _

/10

▶ 511 ~ 520

1	거의	_ _ _ _ _ _ t	6	장소	_ _ _ _ _
2	작은	s _ _ _ _	7	~보다 위에	_ _ _ _ e
3	관심을 가지다, 상관하다	c _ _ _	8	건너다	c _ _ _ _
4	마을	v _ _ _ _ _ _	9	핀, 클립	_ _ _ p
5	표면	s _ _ _ _ _ _	10	침실	b _ _ _ _ _ _

/10

▶ 521 ~ 530

1	새장; 우리	_ _ _ _	6	진짜의	r _ _ _
2	주된, 주요한	m _ _ _	7	다리	b _ _ _ _ _
3	수영하다	s _ _ _	8	이미, 벌써	a _ _ _ _ _ _
4	~에 반대하여 [맞서]	a _ _ _ _ _ _	9	여행; 여행하다	t _ _ _ _ _
5	페인트; 페인트를 칠하다	_ _ _ _ _	10	사슬, 쇠줄	c _ _ _ _ _

/10

531 ~ 540 ▷

1	가지고 가다; 잡다	t _ _ _
2	뼈	b _ _ _
3	~한 맛이 나다; 맛	t _ _ _ _
4	환영하다	w _ _ _ _ _ _
5	카트, 손수레	_ _ _ t

6	이모, 고모	a _ _ _
7	~때문에	b _ _ _ _ _ _
8	식당, 레스토랑	_ _ _ _ _ _ _ _ _ _
9	(성인) 여자	w _ _ _ _
10	도시	c _ _ _

/10

541 ~ 550 ▷

1	항공사	_ _ _ _ _ _ e
2	길, 방법	w _ _
3	지불하다	_ _ y
4	놓다, 두다	_ _ y
5	(음악) 밴드	b _ _ _

6	떨어져	a _ _ _
7	지하철	_ _ _ _ _ _
8	일기	d _ _ _ _
9	학원	_ _ _ _ _ _ _
10	주의 깊게	_ _ _ _ _ _ _ _ _

/10

501~550 Review | 정답

501~510	511~520	521~530	531~540	541~550
1 area	1 almost	1 cage	1 take	1 airline
2 bake	2 small	2 main	2 bone	2 way
3 park	3 care	3 swim	3 taste	3 pay
4 important	4 village	4 against	4 welcome	4 lay
5 march	5 surface	5 paint	5 cart	5 band
6 basketball	6 place	6 real	6 aunt	6 away
7 ant	7 above	7 bridge	7 because	7 subway
8 base	8 cross	8 already	8 restaurant	8 diary
9 sit	9 clip	9 travel	9 woman	9 academy
10 notebook	10 bedroom	10 chain	10 city	10 carefully

Voca Itself

🎙 **Match Spellings & Sounds** 녹음을 듣고 따라 말해보세요.

sleepy	pencil	science	chance	carry
street	ago	basic	bicycle	copy

Match Spellings & Meanings 우리말 뜻이 암기될 때까지 단어를 빈칸에 반복해서 쓰세요.

🎤 551	**sleepy**	▷		졸리는
🎤 552	**pencil**	▷		연필
🎤 553	**science**	▷		과학
🎤 554	**chance**	▷		기회
🎤 555	**carry**	▷		옮기다
🎤 556	**street**	▷		거리, 도로
🎤 557	**ago**	▷		(얼마의 시간) 전에
🎤 558	**basic**	▷		기초의, 기본적인
🎤 559	**bicycle**	▷		자전거
🎤 560	**copy**	▷		복사하다

🔊 **Link to Sounds!** 다음 단어의 발음에 주의하여 빈칸에 들어갈 철자를 쓰세요.

pen＿＿il　　＿＿arry　　basi＿＿　　bi＿＿y＿＿le　　＿＿opy

Voca in Stories

정답과 해설 p.3

⭐ 몇몇 단어들은 문장에서 쓰일 때 형태나 의미가 조금 바뀌기도 해요.

555 • He is **carry**ing 그는 옮기고 있다

Fill in the Blanks 다음 글을 읽고 빈칸에 가장 알맞은 단어를 넣어 보세요.

1
I started to learn
Chinese.
Now I can just speak
_____ Chinese.

2
A long time _____,
there lived a prince
in a castle. One day,
a <u>witch</u> turned him
마녀
into a frog.

3
I love _____. I like to read
stories about great scientists like
<u>Thomas Edison</u>.
토머스 에디슨

4

Ben was <u>absent</u> from school for
결석한
two days. "Can I _____ your
notebook?" Ben asked.

5
Jenny played a computer game with Mike.
"I won!" Jenny said. "Jenny, give me another
_____, please?" said Mike.

6
Do you have any _____s?
I didn't bring my _____ case
today.

7
Tom is _____ a heavy box. He
needs to take an elevator. Oh, no!
The building has no elevator!

8
Jason is riding his _____
along the river. He rides every day
for exercise.

9
The new library is on
this _____.
So, you need to go
straight.

10
I am very _____.
I didn't sleep well
last night. My baby
sister cried all night
because she was
sick.

Voca Itself

🎧 **Match Spellings & Sounds** 녹음을 듣고 따라 말해보세요.

change	such	cheap	chocolate	each
end	fall	hello	job	machine

Match Spellings & Meanings 우리말 뜻이 암기될 때까지 단어를 빈칸에 반복해서 쓰세요.

🎤 561	change	▷		바꾸다
🎤 562	such	▷		그러한
🎤 563	cheap	▷		저렴한, 값싼
🎤 564	chocolate	▷		초콜릿
🎤 565	each	▷		각각의
🎤 566	end	▷		끝; 끝나다
🎤 567	fall	▷		떨어지다
🎤 568	hello	▷		안녕
🎤 569	job	▷		일, 직장
🎤 570	machine	▷		기계

🔊 **Link to Sounds!** 다음 단어의 발음에 주의하여 빈칸에 들어갈 철자를 쓰세요.

____ange   su____   ____eap   ____ocolate   ea____   ma____ine

Voca in Stories

정답과 해설 p.4

⭐ 몇몇 단어들은 문장에서 쓰일 때 형태나 의미가 조금 바뀌기도 해요.

561 • She **changed** 그녀는 바꾸었다   567 • They are **falling** 그들은 떨어지고 있다
566 • It **ended** 그것은 끝났다

🖊 **Fill in the Blanks**   다음 글을 읽고 빈칸에 가장 알맞은 단어를 넣어 보세요.

1
Don't say _____ things. It's rude.
예의 없는
Speak kindly.

2
Kate has three colored pencils. _____ color is different. They are blue, purple, and brown.

3
There are many _____ s in a factory. People at the factory can work faster with those _____ s.

4
"Vegetables are _____ here," Jake's mother said. "I paid more at the other store. I should come here more often."

5
Valentine's Day is coming soon.
밸런타인데이
I will make some _____.
I want to give it to my dad.

6
Jane _____ her hairstyle. "Jane, you look great," said her friend. Jane feels good about it.

7
John's birthday party started at 1 p.m. and _____ three hours later. Everyone left his house at 4 o'clock.

8
The red and yellow leaves are _____ on the ground. Winter is almost here.

9
My father is a police officer. His _____ is important.

10
"Mom, this is my friend, Jenny," said Lucy.
"_____, Jenny. Nice to meet you," said Lucy's mom.

Voca Itself

🎤 **Match Spellings & Sounds** 녹음을 듣고 따라 말해보세요.

beside	branch	collect	correct	doll
draw	effect	farm	flag	subject

Match Spellings & Meanings 우리말 뜻이 암기될 때까지 단어를 빈칸에 반복해서 쓰세요.

🎤 571	beside	▷		～옆에
🎤 572	branch	▷		나뭇가지
🎤 573	collect	▷		모으다
🎤 574	correct	▷		정확한
🎤 575	doll	▷		인형
🎤 576	draw	▷		그리다
🎤 577	effect	▷		영향; 효과
🎤 578	farm	▷		농장
🎤 579	flag	▷		깃발
🎤 580	subject	▷		과목

🎧 **Link to Sounds!** 다음 단어의 발음에 주의하여 빈칸에 들어갈 철자를 쓰세요.

colle_____   corre_____   effe_____   subje_____

Voca in Stories

⭐ 몇몇 단어들은 문장에서 쓰일 때 형태나 의미가 조금 바뀌기도 해요.

576 •She drew 그녀는 그렸다

🔵 **Fill in the Blanks** 다음 글을 읽고 빈칸에 가장 알맞은 단어를 넣어 보세요.

1 Tom likes to _____ toy cars. He wants to get another one this Christmas.

2 Kate _____ something on the school wall. Her teacher saw it. Now, she has to erase the drawing.
지우다

3 Jenny has many _____s. But she doesn't play with them anymore. She is too old for that.

4 All the leaves fell from the tree. Now, the _____es of the tree have no leaves.

5 My grandfather has a small _____ in the country. There are animals like cows and pigs on his farm.

6 Jason likes math. That is his favorite _____ in school. So, he always gets a good grade in math class.

7 I was not healthy before. But I exercised a lot. And now I'm very healthy.
건강한
That is the _____ of exercise.

8 There is a green _____. When the teacher raises it, the race starts. Are you ready?

9 Mary didn't get the _____ answer. She got zero points.

10 "Dad, where is your car?" asked Ben. "It is _____ that building over there," said his dad. "Oh, now I can see it."

Voca Itself

🎙 **Match Spellings & Sounds** 녹음을 듣고 따라 말해보세요.

block	backpack	pocket	as	check
pick	rock	shock	sock	truck

Match Spellings & Meanings 우리말 뜻이 암기될 때까지 단어를 빈칸에 반복해서 쓰세요.

🎙 581	**block**	▷		구역, 블록
🎙 582	**backpack**	▷		배낭, 책가방
🎙 583	**pocket**	▷		주머니
🎙 584	**as**	▷		~처럼
🎙 585	**check**	▷		수표
🎙 586	**pick**	▷		따다, 줍다
🎙 587	**rock**	▷		돌, 바위
🎙 588	**shock**	▷		충격
🎙 589	**sock**	▷		양말
🎙 590	**truck**	▷		트럭

🔊 **Link to Sounds!** 다음 단어의 발음에 주의하여 빈칸에 들어갈 철자를 쓰세요.

blo____   po____et   pi____   so____   tru____

Voca in Stories

⭐ 몇몇 단어들은 문장에서 쓰일 때 형태나 의미가 조금 바뀌기도 해요.

586 • He **picks** 그는 딴다

Fill in the Blanks 다음 글을 읽고 빈칸에 가장 알맞은 단어를 넣어 보세요.

1
My father learned to drive a _____.
He always wanted to be a driver.

2
Go two _____s.
You will see the bookstore. You need to hurry up. It will close soon.

3
I am wearing rain boots. But my _____ got all wet. Oh, no! There is a hole in my right boot.

4
It is a cold day. Ben keeps his hands in his _____s.
"Tomorrow I should wear gloves."

5
It is Halloween. I am dressed up _____ Superman. My sister is dressed up _____ a princess.

6
There were beautiful _____s all over the mountain. Some _____s looked like elephants.

7
Tom cannot wear a _____.
So, his brother is carrying his _____ to school for him.

8
Jack's father grows apples on his farm. Jack sometimes helps his father. He _____ apples and puts them in a basket.

9
People in other countries use _____s. They pay bills with them.
고지서, 청구서

10
There was a fire in that building yesterday. It was a _____!
Thankfully, no one
다행스럽게도
got hurt.

Voca Itself

🎧 **Match Spellings & Sounds** 녹음을 듣고 따라 말해보세요.

enjoy	enter	below	brake	cinema
comedy	complete	contest	energy	engine

✏️ **Match Spellings & Meanings** 우리말 뜻이 암기될 때까지 단어를 빈칸에 반복해서 쓰세요.

🎤	591	**enjoy**	▷	즐기다
🎤	592	**enter**	▷	들어가다
🎤	593	**below**	▷	~보다 아래에
🎤	594	**brake**	▷	브레이크, 제동 장치
🎤	595	**cinema**	▷	영화관
🎤	596	**comedy**	▷	코미디
🎤	597	**complete**	▷	완료하다; 완전한
🎤	598	**contest**	▷	대회
🎤	599	**energy**	▷	에너지, 활기
🎤	600	**engine**	▷	엔진

🎧 **Link to Sounds!** 다음 단어의 발음에 주의하여 빈칸에 들어갈 철자를 쓰세요.

____njoy   ____nter   brak____   cin____ma   com____dy   ____ngine

Voca in Stories

⭐ 몇몇 단어들은 문장에서 쓰일 때 형태나 의미가 조금 바뀌기도 해요.

591 •She **enjoy**ed 그녀는 즐겼다   592 •They are **enter**ing 그들은 들어가고 있다

Fill in the Blanks 다음 글을 읽고 빈칸에 가장 알맞은 단어를 넣어 보세요.

1 Nate loves good _____ movies.
He laughs a lot when he watches them.
They <u>cheer</u> him <u>up</u>.
기운 나게 하다

2 The school is having a writing _____ next week. Only two students from each class can enter.

3 Amy was driving. Suddenly a cat came out on the road. She pushed hard on the _____ s! <u>Fortunately</u>, the cat wasn't hurt.
다행히

4 Jenny likes to go to the _____ . She likes to watch movies on a big screen with popcorn.

5 "The test is over now," the teacher says. But Tom didn't _____ the test yet. He has one question left.

6 I live on the 5th floor. Mike lives _____ my house. Mike lives on the 4th floor.

7 Plants get _____ from the sun. They need the sun's _____ to grow.

8 Many people are _____ the building in a long line. A new restaurant is in there. It is really popular.

9 "The movie was great," Mike said. "Yes. I _____ it!" Sara said.

10 Mary's mother is at a <u>gas station</u>. 주유소
She turns off the _____ .
Then she puts gas in her car.

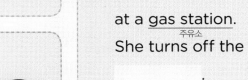

551~600 Review

✏️ **Test Yourself!** 다음 우리말을 뜻하는 영어 단어를 빈칸에 쓰고 아래 표에서 정답을 확인하세요.

551 ~ 560 ▷

1	옮기다	c _ _ _ _ _
2	연필	_ _ _ _ _ _
3	기초의, 기본적인	b _ _ _ _
4	졸리는	_ _ _ _ _ _
5	기회	_ _ _ _ _ _

6	과학	_ _ _ _ _ _ _
7	거리, 도로	s _ _ _ _ _
8	복사하다	_ _ _ _
9	자전거	b _ _ _ _ _ _
10	(얼마의 시간) ~전에	a _ _

/10

561 ~ 570 ▷

1	각각의	_ _ _ _
2	끝; 끝나다	_ _ _
3	저렴한, 값싼	c _ _ _ _
4	기계	m _ _ _ _ _ _
5	안녕	_ _ _ _ _

6	바꾸다	_ h _ _ _ _
7	일, 직장	_ _ b
8	초콜릿	_ _ _ _ _ _ _ _ _
9	떨어지다	f _ _ _
10	그러한	_ _ _ h

/10

571 ~ 580 ▷

1	모으다	_ _ _ _ _ _ _
2	인형	d _ _ _
3	~옆에	b _ _ _ _ _
4	과목	_ _ _ _ _ _ _
5	그리다	_ _ _ w

6	정확한	c _ _ _ _ _ _
7	농장	_ _ _ m
8	나뭇가지	b _ _ _ _ _
9	깃발	f _ _ _
10	영향; 효과	e _ _ _ _ _ _

/10

581 ~ 590 ▷

1	따다, 줍다	_ i _ _	6	수표	_ _ _ _ k
2	주머니	_ _ _ _ _ _	7	충격	_ _ _ _ _
3	~처럼	_ _	8	배낭, 책가방	b _ _ _ _ _ _ _
4	양말	_ _ _ _	9	트럭	_ _ _ _ _
5	구역, 블록	_ _ _ _ _	10	돌, 바위	_ _ _ k

/10

591 ~ 600 ▷

1	코미디	_ _ _ _ _ y	6	즐기다	_ _ _ _ _
2	에너지, 활기	_ _ _ _ _ _	7	브레이크, 제동 장치	b _ _ _ _
3	들어가다	_ _ _ _ r	8	대회	_ _ _ _ _ _ t
4	완료하다; 완전한	c _ _ _ _ _ _ _	9	영화관	c _ _ _ _ _
5	엔진	_ _ _ _ _ _	10	~보다 아래에	b _ _ _ _

/10

551~600 Review | 정답

551~560	561~570	571~580	581~590	591~600
1 carry	1 each	1 collect	1 pick	1 comedy
2 pencil	2 end	2 doll	2 pocket	2 energy
3 basic	3 cheap	3 beside	3 as	3 enter
4 sleepy	4 machine	4 subject	4 sock	4 complete
5 chance	5 hello	5 draw	5 block	5 engine
6 science	6 change	6 correct	6 check	6 enjoy
7 street	7 job	7 farm	7 shock	7 brake
8 copy	8 chocolate	8 branch	8 backpack	8 contest
9 bicycle	9 fall	9 flag	9 truck	9 cinema
10 ago	10 such	10 effect	10 rock	10 below

Voca Itself

🎧 **Match Spellings & Sounds** 녹음을 듣고 따라 말해보세요.

sweet	agree	bee	cheese	engineer
keep	seed	speed	teen	tree

🎤 **Match Spellings & Meanings** 우리말 뜻이 암기될 때까지 단어를 빈칸에 반복해서 쓰세요.

🎙 601	**sweet**	▶		달콤한, 단
🎙 602	**agree**	▶		동의하다
🎙 603	**bee**	▶		벌
🎙 604	**cheese**	▶		치즈
🎙 605	**engineer**	▶		엔지니어, 기술자
🎙 606	**keep**	▶		(계속) 가지고 있다
🎙 607	**seed**	▶		씨, 씨앗
🎙 608	**speed**	▶		속도
🎙 609	**teen**	▶		십 대
🎙 610	**tree**	▶		나무

🔊 **Link to Sounds!** 다음 단어의 발음에 주의하여 빈칸에 들어갈 철자를 쓰세요.

sw___t   b___   ch___se   k___p   t___n   tr___

Voca in Stories

⭐ 몇몇 단어들은 문장에서 쓰일 때 형태나 의미가 조금 바뀌기도 해요.

602 ・She **agree**s 그녀는 동의한다   606 ・She **keep**s 그녀는 가지고 있다

✎ **Fill in the Blanks** 다음 글을 읽고 빈칸에 가장 알맞은 단어를 넣어 보세요.

1 Jenny is having a piece of cake. "This is really good! The strawberries and the cream are really _____. I like it."

2 Slow down! You are driving at a high _____.
It's too dangerous!

3 I planted a _____ in the garden. I <u>watered</u> it every day. Now it is a beautiful flower.
물을 주었다

4 My family loves _____.
We eat it on toast and pizza.

5 Ben knows everything about computers. In the future, he wants to become a computer _____.

6 _____s do many things. They make honey. Plants can make seeds because _____s help them.

7 There are many _____s in the forest. Those _____s make fresh and clean air.

8 "Let's have a party for Mom. You get flowers, and I will get a cake," said John. "Great!
I _____ with your plan," Sara said.

9 Mary _____ her old toys in boxes. She doesn't play with them anymore. So, she puts the boxes under her bed.

10 My cousin is in her _____s now. She is fifteen years old. She goes to middle school.

Voca Itself

🔊 **Match Spellings & Sounds** 녹음을 듣고 따라 말해보세요.

ice cream	bread	dead	heat	heaven
instead	jeans	lead	peace	speak

Match Spellings & Meanings 우리말 뜻이 암기될 때까지 단어를 빈칸에 반복해서 쓰세요.

🎤 611	**ice cream**	▷	아이스크림
🎤 612	**bread**	▷	빵
🎤 613	**dead**	▷	죽은
🎤 614	**heat**	▷	열, 뜨거움
🎤 615	**heaven**	▷	천국
🎤 616	**instead**	▷	대신에
🎤 617	**jeans**	▷	청바지
🎤 618	**lead**	▷	인도하다, 안내하다
🎤 619	**peace**	▷	평화
🎤 620	**speak**	▷	말하다

🔊 **Link to Sounds!** 다음 단어의 발음에 주의하여 빈칸에 들어갈 철자를 쓰세요.

ice cr____m   h____t   j____ns   l____d   p____ce   sp____k

Voca in Stories

⭐ 몇몇 단어들은 문장에서 쓰일 때 형태나 의미가 조금 바뀌기도 해요.

618 · She is **lead**ing 그녀는 인도하고 있다
· She **led** 그녀는 인도했다

🔵 **Fill in the Blanks** 다음 글을 읽고 빈칸에 가장 알맞은 단어를 넣어 보세요.

1
I don't want the cookie. I want the candy _____ .

2
Jenny's grandmother is living, but her grandfather is _____ . She misses him.

3
It is very hot in here. Where is this _____ coming from? The heater was <u>on</u> all day.
(전원이) 켜진

4
Little girls and boys are singing happily. Their song sounds beautiful. They look like angels from _____ .

5
 You can have _____ and milk or rice. Just don't skip your breakfast.

6
It is so <u>noisy</u> here! Sorry, what did
시끄러운
you say? I cannot hear you.
Can you _____ louder?

7
 "Do you want your vanilla _____ in a cone or cup?" Lucy's mom said. "I want it in a cone, please," said Lucy.

8
I love to wear _____ . You can wear anything with them. They look good with any clothes in any color.

9
Mary is _____ us through the crowd. "Come on, we are almost there. Just <u>follow</u> me."
따라오다

10
The war between the countries is over now. They just want _____ .

Voca Itself

🎙 **Match Spellings & Sounds** 녹음을 듣고 따라 말해보세요.

later	anger	apartment	clerk	concert
cover	determine	farmer	member	paper

Match Spellings & Meanings 우리말 뜻이 암기될 때까지 단어를 빈칸에 반복해서 쓰세요.

🎙 621	**later**	▷		나중에
🎙 622	**anger**	▷		화, 분노
🎙 623	**apartment**	▷		아파트
🎙 624	**clerk**	▷		직원, 점원
🎙 625	**concert**	▷		연주회, 콘서트
🎙 626	**cover**	▷		가리다, 덮다
🎙 627	**determine**	▷		결정하다
🎙 628	**farmer**	▷		농부
🎙 629	**member**	▷		구성원, 회원
🎙 630	**paper**	▷		종이

🎧 **Link to Sounds!** 다음 단어의 발음에 주의하여 빈칸에 들어갈 철자를 쓰세요.

lat____   cl__k   conc___t   cov____   pap____

Voca **in Stories**

⭐ 몇몇 단어들은 문장에서 쓰일 때 형태나 의미가 조금 바뀌기도 해요.

627 •They **determined** 그들은 결정했다

Fill in the Blanks 다음 글을 읽고 빈칸에 가장 알맞은 단어를 넣어 보세요.

1
"Can I help you?"
said the _____.
"Yes, please. I am
<u>looking for</u> some
　　　　찾고 있다
jackets," said Ben.

2
My uncle will marry
his girlfriend next
year. They already
_____ the
date for the wedding.

3
Tim is going to a _____. He will listen
to his favorite songs. He wants to sing along,
too. He is so excited.

4
I live in an _____
building. My _____ is
on the 8th floor.

5
You need to _____ your bike.
It will rain soon. The bike will get
wet in the rain.

6
I heard _____ in my mom's
voice. She was really mad because
I lied. Will she forgive me?

7
My grandfather was a _____
before. He grew rice.

8

Jane wants to draw something.
She has a pencil and an eraser.
But she doesn't have _____.
Does anyone have any?

9
"John is the new
_____ of
the team. Please
welcome him," said
the <u>coach</u>.
　　　코치

10
"Are you busy now?"
asked Mary. "I have
to leave now. I will
call you _____,
okay?" said Tom.

631~640 words

Voca Itself

🎈 Match Spellings & Sounds 녹음을 듣고 따라 말해보세요.

bubble	control	factory	fantastic	fat
grass	hundred	ice	life	off

Match Spellings & Meanings 우리말 뜻이 암기될 때까지 단어를 빈칸에 반복해서 쓰세요.

🎤 631	**bubble**	▷		거품
🎤 632	**control**	▷		통제하다
🎤 633	**factory**	▷		공장
🎤 634	**fantastic**	▷		환상적인
🎤 635	**fat**	▷		뚱뚱한, 살찐
🎤 636	**grass**	▷		잔디, 풀
🎤 637	**hundred**	▷		백, 100
🎤 638	**ice**	▷		얼음
🎤 639	**life**	▷		삶, 생명
🎤 640	**off**	▷		멀리, 떨어져

🎧 **Link to Sounds!** 다음 단어의 발음에 주의하여 빈칸에 들어갈 철자를 쓰세요.

____actory   ____antastic   ____at   li____e   o____

Voca **in Stories**

정답과 해설 **p.6**

⭐ 몇몇 단어들은 문장에서 쓰일 때 형태나 의미가 조금 바뀌기도 해요.

632 • She **control**s 그녀는 통제한다

💡 **Fill in the Blanks** 다음 글을 읽고 빈칸에 가장 알맞은 단어를 넣어 보세요.

1 Children are running around in the classroom. The teacher needs to _____ them.

2 That trip was _____. I had so much fun there. The food was great, too.

3 Could you put some _____ in my water, please? It is not cold enough for me.

4 Tom used too much shampoo in the shower. There were _____s everywhere.

5 The fox ate too many grapes. He is _____ now. He cannot jump over the <u>fence</u>. Oh, no!
울타리
The farmer will be here soon.

6 Jake wants to visit a chocolate _____. He wants to see the chocolate machines.

7 **100** "What is 80 plus 20?" Lucy's sister said, "A _____?" "That's correct," said Lucy.

8 My mother wants to live a <u>healthy</u> _____.
건강한
She exercises every day. She eats lots of vegetables and fruit.

9 The _____ was green before. But now it is yellow. We didn't have enough rain last summer.

10 Please take your feet _____ the table. It is very <u>rude</u>. Besides,
예의 없는
your feet are dirty!

Voca Itself

🎈 **Match Spellings & Sounds** 녹음을 듣고 따라 말해보세요.

forgive	singer	beat	college	danger
dialogue	frog	gate	gentleman	giraffe

Match Spellings & Meanings 우리말 뜻이 암기될 때까지 단어를 빈칸에 반복해서 쓰세요.

🎤 641	**forgive**	▷		용서하다
🎤 642	**singer**	▷		가수
🎤 643	**beat**	▷		이기다; 때리다
🎤 644	**college**	▷		대학
🎤 645	**danger**	▷		위험
🎤 646	**dialogue**	▷		대화
🎤 647	**frog**	▷		개구리
🎤 648	**gate**	▷		대문, 출입문
🎤 649	**gentleman**	▷		신사
🎤 650	**giraffe**	▷		기린

🎈 **Link to Sounds!** 다음 단어의 발음에 주의하여 빈칸에 들어갈 철자를 쓰세요.

for___ive   sin___er   colle___e   dan___er   fro___

Voca in Stories

정답과 해설 p.7

⭐ 몇몇 단어들은 문장에서 쓰일 때 형태나 의미가 조금 바뀌기도 해요.

641 •She forgave 그녀는 용서했다   643 •They beat 그들은 이겼다

🔵 **Fill in the Blanks** 다음 글을 읽고 빈칸에 가장 알맞은 단어를 넣어 보세요.

1
"I am so sorry," said
the boy.
"It's okay," said
the woman. She
_____ the boy.

2
Jake's team
_____ Mary's
team. The score was
3 to 2. Jake was really
happy and proud.

3

My uncle is a _____. He
is nice to everyone. He always says,
"After you." Many people like him.
먼저 가세요

4
This bottle says, "_____."
It must be dangerous. Don't touch
it. Why is it here? What's inside?

5

The _____ is the tallest animal
in the world. It has a long neck and
long legs. It is about 5 meters tall.

6
My cousin finishes high school this year.
Next year, he will go to _____.
What will he study there?

7
The school _____ is closing.
John needs to run!

8

_____s have four legs. Their
hind legs grow before their front legs.
뒷다리
I learned that from science class.

9
Tim overhears the
우연히 듣다
_____ between
his dad and mom.
They are talking
about Tim's brother.

10
The _____ is
having a concert
next week. But he is
sick with a cold.
Can he really sing?

601~650 Review

🖊 **Test Yourself!** 다음 우리말을 뜻하는 영어 단어를 빈칸에 쓰고 아래 표에서 정답을 확인하세요.

601 ~ 610 ▷

1	(계속) 가지고 있다	_ _ _ p
2	달콤한, 단	_ _ _ _ _
3	나무	_ _ _ _
4	동의하다	a _ _ _ _ _
5	속도	s _ _ _ _

6	벌	b _ _
7	엔지니어, 기술자	_ _ _ _ _ _ _ _
8	십 대	_ _ _ _
9	씨, 씨앗	s _ _ _
10	치즈	_ _ _ _ _ _

/10

611 ~ 620 ▷

1	청바지	_ _ _ _ _
2	인도하다, 안내하다	_ _ _ _
3	아이스크림	i _ _ c _ _ _ _ _
4	말하다	s _ _ _ _
5	대신에	_ _ _ _ _ _ d

6	빵	_ _ _ _ _
7	평화	p _ _ _ _
8	열, 뜨거움	h _ _ _
9	천국	h _ _ _ _ _
10	죽은	d _ _ _

/10

621 ~ 630 ▷

1	가리다, 덮다	c _ _ _ _
2	농부	_ _ _ _ _ _
3	나중에	l _ _ _ _
4	종이	p _ _ _ _
5	결정하다	d _ _ _ _ _ _ _ _

6	화, 분노	_ _ _ _ _
7	직원, 점원	c _ _ _ _
8	구성원, 회원	m _ _ _ _ _
9	아파트	_ _ _ _ _ m _ _ _
10	연주회, 콘서트	_ _ _ _ _ _ t

/10

631 ~ 640 ▷

1	환상적인	f _ _ _ _ _ _ _ _
2	얼음	_ _ _
3	멀리, 떨어져	o _ _
4	거품	b _ _ _ _ _
5	뚱뚱한, 살찐	f _ _

6	공장	f _ _ _ _ _ _
7	백, 100	h _ _ _ _ _ _
8	통제하다	c _ _ _ _ _ _
9	삶, 생명	_ _ _ _
10	잔디, 풀	_ _ _ _ _

/10

641 ~ 650 ▷

1	신사	_ _ _ _ _ _ _ _ _
2	개구리	_ _ _ _
3	용서하다	f _ _ _ _ _ _
4	기린	g _ _ _ _ _ _
5	위험	_ _ _ _ _ _

6	이기다; 때리다	b _ _ _
7	대화	d _ _ _ _ _ _ _
8	가수	_ _ _ _ _ _
9	대문, 출입문	g _ _ _
10	대학	c _ _ _ _ _ _

/10

601~650 Review | 정답

601~610	611~620	621~630	631~640	641~650
1 keep	1 jeans	1 cover	1 fantastic	1 gentleman
2 sweet	2 lead	2 farmer	2 ice	2 frog
3 tree	3 ice cream	3 later	3 off	3 forgive
4 agree	4 speak	4 paper	4 bubble	4 giraffe
5 speed	5 instead	5 determine	5 fat	5 danger
6 bee	6 bread	6 anger	6 factory	6 beat
7 engineer	7 peace	7 clerk	7 hundred	7 dialogue
8 teen	8 heat	8 member	8 control	8 singer
9 seed	9 heaven	9 apartment	9 life	9 gate
10 cheese	10 dead	10 concert	10 grass	10 college

Voca Itself

🎤 **Match Spellings & Sounds** 녹음을 듣고 따라 말해보세요.

night	straight	light	might	brave
bright	dance	hunt	through	weight

Match Spellings & Meanings 우리말 뜻이 암기될 때까지 단어를 빈칸에 반복해서 쓰세요.

🎤	651	**night**	▷		밤
🎤	652	**straight**	▷		똑바로
🎤	653	**light**	▷		(전깃)불, (전)등
🎤	654	**might**	▷		~일지도 모른다, ~일수도 있다
🎤	655	**brave**	▷		용감한
🎤	656	**bright**	▷		밝은
🎤	657	**dance**	▷		춤을 추다; 춤
🎤	658	**hunt**	▷		사냥하다
🎤	659	**through**	▷		~을 통해
🎤	660	**weight**	▷		무게

🔊 **Link to Sounds!** 다음 단어의 발음에 주의하여 빈칸에 들어갈 철자를 쓰세요.

ni___t   strai___t   li___t   mi___t   bri___t   throu___   wei___t

Voca in Stories

정답과 해설 p.7

⭐ 몇몇 단어들은 문장에서 쓰일 때 형태나 의미가 조금 바뀌기도 해요.

654 •He might 그는 ~일지도 모른다

🔖 **Fill in the Blanks** 다음 글을 읽고 빈칸에 가장 알맞은 단어를 넣어 보세요.

1
Ben _____ be late for school. He woke up late this morning. He needs to hurry.

2
The new tunnel is very long. When the train goes _____ the tunnel, it is really dark inside the train.

3
Santa Claus only comes late at _____. Go to bed now. Or he 그렇지 않으면
won't come.

4

Jake's father catches a big fish. The _____ is 5 kilograms. That is a heavy fish!

5
Owls can see well in the dark with their big 부엉이
eyes. They _____ other animals for food at night.

6
Police officers are _____. They catch bad people. Fire fighters are _____, too. They fight fires and save lives.

7
It is so dark. Where is the switch? I can't see anything! I need to turn on the _____. 켜다

8

Just go _____ and turn left at the bookstore. It is not too far. You will be there in 5 minutes.

9
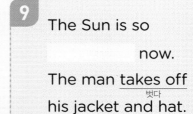
The Sun is so _____ now. The man takes off 벗다
his jacket and hat.

10
Everyone started to _____ to the band's music. They are having so much fun!

Voca Itself

🎙 **Match Spellings & Sounds** 녹음을 듣고 따라 말해보세요.

boring	chicken	cousin	finally	habit
hospital	into	invite	island	kill

Match Spellings & Meanings 우리말 뜻이 암기될 때까지 단어를 빈칸에 반복해서 쓰세요.

🎙 661	**boring**	▷		재미없는, 지루한
🎙 662	**chicken**	▷		닭; 닭고기
🎙 663	**cousin**	▷		사촌
🎙 664	**finally**	▷		마침내
🎙 665	**habit**	▷		습관
🎙 666	**hospital**	▷		병원
🎙 667	**into**	▷		~ 안으로
🎙 668	**invite**	▷		초대하다
🎙 669	**island**	▷		섬
🎙 670	**kill**	▷		죽이다

🎧 **Link to Sounds!** 다음 단어의 발음에 주의하여 빈칸에 들어갈 철자를 쓰세요.

bor____ng   cous____n   f____nally   hab____t   ____sland

Voca in Stories

정답과 해설 p.8

⭐ 몇몇 단어들은 문장에서 쓰일 때 형태나 의미가 조금 바뀌기도 해요.

668
- He **invites** 그는 초대한다
- He **invited** 그는 초대했다

Fill in the Blanks 다음 글을 읽고 빈칸에 가장 알맞은 단어를 넣어 보세요.

1
Mike will have a birthday party. He wants to _____ many friends. His mom agrees.

2
Jane, you didn't finish your homework yet. Go _____ your room and finish it now.

3

I am in my uncle's house now. But it is so _____ here. There are no kids, no games, and no playground.

4
Kate's mom is a nurse. She works at a _____. She is always busy at work. But she loves her job.

5
There is a <u>mosquito</u> in my room! I can't go 모기 to sleep! I have to _____ it. Where is it? Where did it go?

6
Lucy's family went to a small _____ by boat. It was beautiful.

7
There were too many cars on the road! Tom _____ arrived after three hours.

8
_____s are birds. Can _____s fly? Most of them cannot fly high. So, you won't see them in the sky.

9
My aunt just <u>had a</u> 아기를 낳았다 <u>baby</u>. Now I have a baby _____. I am so excited. I want to meet her soon.

10
"Jenny, you need to stop shaking your leg. It is a bad _____," said Mom to Jenny.

Voca Itself

🔵 **Match Spellings & Sounds** 녹음을 듣고 따라 말해보세요.

by	shirt	fly	birth	catch
circle	clever	especially	skirt	thirst

Match Spellings & Meanings 우리말 뜻이 암기될 때까지 단어를 빈칸에 반복해서 쓰세요

🎤 671	**by**	▶	~옆에
🎤 672	**shirt**	▶	셔츠
🎤 673	**fly**	▶	날다
🎤 674	**birth**	▶	탄생, 출생
🎤 675	**catch**	▶	잡다
🎤 676	**circle**	▶	동그라미, 원
🎤 677	**clever**	▶	영리한, 똑똑한
🎤 678	**especially**	▶	특히
🎤 679	**skirt**	▶	치마
🎤 680	**thirst**	▶	갈증, 목마름

🎧 **Link to Sounds!** 다음 단어의 발음에 주의하여 빈칸에 들어갈 철자를 쓰세요.

sh____t　　b____th　　c____cle　　sk____t　　th____st

Voca in Stories

정답과 해설 p.8

⭐ 몇몇 단어들은 문장에서 쓰일 때 형태나 의미가 조금 바뀌기도 해요.

675 · He **catch**es 그는 잡는다

✐ Fill in the Blanks 다음 글을 읽고 빈칸에 가장 알맞은 단어를 넣어 보세요.

1 My grandfather lives _____ a small lake. He takes a walk around it every day.

2 This restaurant makes delicious food. The pizza and steak are good. But I _____ like the dessert here.

3 Can pigs _____ ? No, they can't. They are too heavy. And they don't have <u>wings</u>.
날개

4 My dad and I love baseball. We sometimes play together. I <u>throw</u> the
던지다
ball, and he _____ it.

5 My dog had five puppies. They are so cute and lovely. My family is so excited about the _____ of the puppies.

6 The wedding is next week. What should I wear? A _____ or pants? I can't decide.

7 "Rings, pizzas, balls, apples, oranges. What shape are these?" The kids answer, "They are _____ s!"

8 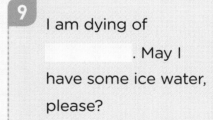 My arms are too long for this _____ . I need to get a bigger one.

9 I am dying of _____ . May I have some ice water, please?

10 Her friends can ask Mary about anything. She knows all the answers! Mary is very _____ .

Voca Itself

🔲 **Match Spellings & Sounds** 녹음을 듣고 따라 말해보세요.

bear	divide	file	glass	lake
list	symbol	wild	world	festival

Match Spellings & Meanings 우리말 뜻이 암기될 때까지 단어를 빈칸에 반복해서 쓰세요

🎤 681	**bear**	▷	곰
🎤 682	**divide**	▷	나누다
🎤 683	**file**	▷	파일
🎤 684	**glass**	▷	유리; 유리잔
🎤 685	**lake**	▷	호수
🎤 686	**list**	▷	목록, 리스트
🎤 687	**symbol**	▷	상징
🎤 688	**wild**	▷	야생의
🎤 689	**world**	▷	세계, 세상
🎤 690	**festival**	▷	축제

🎧 **Link to Sounds!** 다음 단어의 발음에 주의하여 빈칸에 들어갈 철자를 쓰세요.

fi___e ___ake ___ist symbo___ wor___d festiva___

Voca in Stories

정답과 해설 p.8

⭐ 몇몇 단어들은 문장에서 쓰일 때 형태나 의미가 조금 바뀌기도 해요.

682 • He **divided** 그는 나눴다

🔍 **Fill in the Blanks** 다음 글을 읽고 빈칸에 가장 알맞은 단어를 넣어 보세요.

1
When you see a
green cross, what
<u>십자 기호</u>
comes to mind?
It is the _____
of a hospital.

2
My dad keeps his
_____ s on his desk.
They are about his
work. They must be
<u>~임이 틀림없다</u>
very important.

3

Two friends are walking in the forest.
One friend sees a _____. "Look!
It's a _____." He climbs a tree.

4
Can you pass me that _____
over there? I want to drink some
water.

5
Jake made a Christmas present wish
_____. Will he get all of them?
Let's see.

6
There is a small _____ in our town.
In winter, we can skate there. In summer, we
can swim there.

7
I traveled around the _____.
I visited many countries. I ate many
kinds of food.

8
Mary went to a _____ with her
family. She saw a great <u>parade</u>. And there
<u>퍼레이드</u>
were many fun things.

9
There are _____
animals like bears
and wolves in the
forest. You should
be careful.

10
The teacher
_____ the
students into two
teams, a red team
and a blue team.

Voca Itself

🎙 **Match Spellings & Sounds** 녹음을 듣고 따라 말해보세요.

must	cat	seem	moment	beautiful
company	customer	forest	form	jump

Match Spellings & Meanings 우리말 뜻이 암기될 때까지 단어를 빈칸에 반복해서 쓰세요.

🎙 691	**must**	▷		~해야 하다
🎙 692	**cat**	▷		고양이
🎙 693	**seem**	▷		~인 것처럼 보이다
🎙 694	**moment**	▷		잠깐; 순간
🎙 695	**beautiful**	▷		아름다운
🎙 696	**company**	▷		회사
🎙 697	**customer**	▷		손님, 고객
🎙 698	**forest**	▷		숲
🎙 699	**form**	▷		형태
🎙 700	**jump**	▷		뛰다, 점프하다

🎧 **Link to Sounds!** 다음 단어의 발음에 주의하여 빈칸에 들어갈 철자를 쓰세요.

____ust   see____   ____o____ent   custo____er   for____   ju____p

Voca in Stories

정답과 해설 p.9

⭐ 몇몇 단어들은 문장에서 쓰일 때 형태나 의미가 조금 바뀌기도 해요.

693 •He **seem**s 그는 ~인 것처럼 보인다　　700 •They are **jump**ing 그들은 뛰고 있다

🔵 **Fill in the Blanks** 다음 글을 읽고 빈칸에 가장 알맞은 단어를 넣어 보세요.

1 The coffee shop is very popular. Their cake is really good. Many _____s visit there.

2 Jenny _____ finish her homework now. Then she can watch TV.

3 My family likes to go to the _____. We can enjoy the fresh air. It is very relaxing.

4 Kate's father works at a small _____. It is in a big city. So, he has to wake up early to go to work.

5 The kids are _____ around the house. "Can you please stop it? I can't watch TV!"

6 She looks very _____ in that dress. She looks like a princess in a fairy tale.
　　　　　　　　　　　　　　　　　　　동화

7 Can you wait a _____, please? I just need to get my bag from the classroom. Just three minutes!

8 There is a little _____ under the car. It is crying. Meow, meow. Maybe it is hungry.

9 Books are usually rectangles. But
직사각형
some are in different _____s, like circles or triangles.

10 Is he the new student in your class? He _____ nice. We should talk to him first.

651~700 Review

Test Yourself! 다음 우리말을 뜻하는 영어 단어를 빈칸에 쓰고 아래 표에서 정답을 확인하세요.

651 ~ 660

1	무게	w _ _ _ _ _
2	똑바로	_ _ _ _ _ _ _ t
3	(전깃)불, (전)등	_ _ _ _ _
4	밝은	_ _ _ _ _ _
5	~을 통해	t _ _ _ _ _ _

6	춤을 추다; 춤	d _ _ _ _
7	사냥하다	_ _ _ _
8	~일지도 모른다, ~일수도 있다	m _ _ _ _
9	밤	n _ _ _ _
10	용감한	_ _ _ _ _

/10

661 ~ 670

1	습관	h _ _ _ _
2	초대하다	_ _ _ _ _ _
3	사촌	_ _ _ _ _ n
4	재미없는, 지루한	b _ _ _ _ _
5	죽이다	_ _ _ _

6	병원	h _ _ _ _ _ _ _
7	섬	_ _ _ _ _ d
8	마침내	_ _ _ _ _ _ _
9	~ 안으로	_ _ _ o
10	닭; 닭고기	_ _ _ _ _ _ _

/10

671 ~ 680

1	치마	_ _ _ _ _
2	특히	_ _ _ _ _ _ _ _ _ _
3	잡다	c _ _ _ _ _
4	탄생, 출생	b _ _ _ _
5	날다	_ _ _

6	동그라미, 원	c _ _ _ _ _ _
7	영리한, 똑똑한	_ _ _ _ _ r
8	~옆에	b _
9	갈증, 목마름	_ _ _ _ _ _
10	셔츠	_ _ _ _ _

/10

681 ~ 690 ▷

1	상징	s _ _ _ _ _
2	파일	_ _ _ _
3	곰	_ _ _ _
4	축제	f _ _ _ _ _ _ _
5	호수	_ _ _ _

6	야생의	_ _ _ _
7	유리; 유리잔	g _ _ _ _
8	세계, 세상	_ _ _ _ d
9	목록, 리스트	_ _ _ _
10	나누다	d _ _ _ _ _

/10

691 ~ 700 ▷

1	손님, 고객	c _ _ _ _ _ _ _
2	뛰다, 점프하다	_ _ _ _
3	아름다운	b _ _ _ _ _ _ _
4	~인 것처럼 보이다	s _ _ _
5	회사	_ _ _ _ _ _ _

6	형태	f _ _ _
7	잠깐; 순간	m _ _ _ _ _
8	~해야 하다	m _ _ _
9	고양이	_ _ _
10	숲	_ _ _ _ _ t

/10

651~700 Review | 정답

651~660	661~670	671~680	681~690	691~700
1 weight	1 habit	1 skirt	1 symbol	1 customer
2 straight	2 invite	2 especially	2 file	2 jump
3 light	3 cousin	3 catch	3 bear	3 beautiful
4 bright	4 boring	4 birth	4 festival	4 seem
5 through	5 kill	5 fly	5 lake	5 company
6 dance	6 hospital	6 circle	6 wild	6 form
7 hunt	7 island	7 clever	7 glass	7 moment
8 might	8 finally	8 by	8 world	8 must
9 night	9 into	9 thirst	9 list	9 cat
10 brave	10 chicken	10 shirt	10 divide	10 forest

Voca Itself

🎤 **Match Spellings & Sounds** 녹음을 듣고 따라 말해보세요.

ride	over	anyone	brand	even
note	old	P.M./p.m.	pass	picnic

Match Spellings & Meanings 우리말 뜻이 암기될 때까지 단어를 빈칸에 반복해서 쓰세요.

🎤	701	ride	▷	타다
🎤	702	over	▷	~의 위에
🎤	703	anyone	▷	누군가
🎤	704	brand	▷	상표, 브랜드
🎤	705	even	▷	~조차
🎤	706	note	▷	메모, 쪽지
🎤	707	old	▷	나이가 ~인, 나이가 많은
🎤	708	P.M./p.m.	▷	오후
🎤	709	pass	▷	지나가다, 통과하다
🎤	710	picnic	▷	소풍

🎧 **Link to Sounds!** 다음 단어의 발음에 주의하여 빈칸에 들어갈 철자를 쓰세요.

a____yo____e   bra____d   eve____   ____ote   pic____ic

Voca in Stories

⭐ 몇몇 단어들은 문장에서 쓰일 때 형태나 의미가 조금 바뀌기도 해요.

701 •They **rode** 그들은 **탔다**

709 •It **passed** 그것은 **지나갔다**

Fill in the Blanks 다음 글을 읽고 빈칸에 가장 알맞은 단어를 넣어 보세요.

1 Judy is very sick. She cannot ＿＿＿ get up. Her mother says, "You should stay home today."

2 Jane loves Kate's new shoes. So, she asked Kate, "What is the ＿＿＿ name?"

3 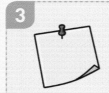 There is a ＿＿＿ on the table. It says, "I went to the supermarket. I will be home before five o'clock."

4 My class will go on a ＿＿＿ next week. We will go to the zoo. There, we will learn about animals.

5 Jason is holding an umbrella ＿＿＿ his head. It will keep him dry.

6 How ＿＿＿ is Kevin? He is 12 years ＿＿＿. His sister is 10 years ＿＿＿.

7 "Can ＿＿＿ answer my question?" Tom raised his hand. "I know the answer. It is twenty-five," said Tom.

8 John's family went to the park. His parents took a walk. John and his brother ＿＿＿ their bicycles.

9 The red car is going too fast. It ＿＿＿ many cars ahead of it. It needs to slow down.

10 My after-school class 방과 후 수업 finishes at 3 ＿＿＿. Can I join you after that? I really want to play soccer, too.

Voca Itself

🎙 **Match Spellings & Sounds** 녹음을 듣고 따라 말해보세요.

interesting	sing	along	evening	hang
king	ring	land	wedding	wing

Match Spellings & Meanings 우리말 뜻이 암기될 때까지 단어를 빈칸에 반복해서 쓰세요.

🎙 711	interesting	▷		재미있는, 흥미로운
🎙 712	sing	▷		노래하다
🎙 713	along	▷		~을 따라
🎙 714	evening	▷		저녁
🎙 715	hang	▷		걸다, 매달다
🎙 716	king	▷		왕
🎙 717	ring	▷		반지
🎙 718	land	▷		땅, 육지
🎙 719	wedding	▷		결혼(식)
🎙 720	wing	▷		날개

🔊 **Link to Sounds!** 다음 단어의 발음에 주의하여 빈칸에 들어갈 철자를 쓰세요.

si____   alo____   eveni____   ha____   ri____   wi____

Voca in Stories

정답과 해설 **p.10**

⭐ 몇몇 단어들은 문장에서 쓰일 때 형태나 의미가 조금 바뀌기도 해요.

715 • He **hang**s 그는 건다
   • He hung 그는 걸었다

Fill in the Blanks 다음 글을 읽고 빈칸에 가장 알맞은 단어를 넣어 보세요.

1 Many people visit the Han River. They ride their bikes or walk _____ the river.

2 The _____ will start soon. Jane, the bride, is wearing a beautiful white dress.
신부

3 The lion is _____ of the animals. They are strong and fast. Other animals are scared of them.

4 Many other birds fly with their _____s. But penguins cannot fly. So, they use their _____s to swim.

5  My dad always _____ his car key on a hook near the door. So, he never forgets it.
고리, 걸이

6 Mary's mother got a _____ for her birthday. It's so beautiful.

7 My mother comes home from work at 7 o'clock in the _____. After that, she cooks dinner for my family.

8 Turtles move slowly on _____.
거북이
But they swim fast in the sea!

9 On this day, people _____ carols.
캐럴
Kids get gifts. Also, it snows sometimes. What is this day?

10 Mike is looking for books to read. Are there any _____ books here?

Voca Itself

🎧 **Match Spellings & Sounds** 녹음을 듣고 따라 말해보세요.

friendly	stand	ground	handsome	husband
triangle	monkey	plant	sand	sound

Match Spellings & Meanings 우리말 뜻이 암기될 때까지 단어를 빈칸에 반복해서 쓰세요.

🎤 721	**friendly**	▶		친절한, 다정한
🎤 722	**stand**	▶		서 있다
🎤 723	**ground**	▶		땅, 땅바닥
🎤 724	**handsome**	▶		멋진, 잘생긴
🎤 725	**husband**	▶		남편
🎤 726	**triangle**	▶		삼각형
🎤 727	**monkey**	▶		원숭이
🎤 728	**plant**	▶		식물
🎤 729	**sand**	▶		모래
🎤 730	**sound**	▶		소리; ~하게 들리다

🔊 **Link to Sounds!** 다음 단어의 발음에 주의하여 빈칸에 들어갈 철자를 쓰세요.

sta____   grou____   mo____ey   pla____

Voca in Stories

정답과 해설 p.10

★ 몇몇 단어들은 문장에서 쓰일 때 형태나 의미가 조금 바뀌기도 해요.

722 •They **stood** 그들은 서 있었다

Fill in the Blanks 다음 글을 읽고 빈칸에 가장 알맞은 단어를 넣어 보세요.

1
There are no seats
on the subway. We
have to _____.
There are too
many people!

2
"Why do you like the
singer?" asked Jane.
"Because he is so
_____.
He has a nice smile."

3
There is a small _____ in the hole.
It has new green leaves now.
When will we see a flower?

4
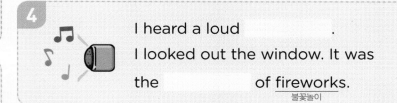
I heard a loud _____.
I looked out the window. It was
the _____ of fireworks.
불꽃놀이

5
Kate is playing on the beach.
The _____ is soft under her
feet.

6
My grandparents loved each other.
They were _____ and wife for 50 years.

7
A little boy dropped his ice
cream on the _____.
He started to cry.

8
'Bi' means two. 'Tri' means three.
So, bicycles have two wheels.
_____s have three sides.

9
Mom, look up there!
A baby _____
is with his mother.
They are eating
bananas in the tree.

10
She is very
_____. She is
nice to everyone.
And she always
smiles.

Voca Itself

🔊 **Match Spellings & Sounds** 녹음을 듣고 따라 말해보세요.

promise	move	also	boss	bottom
forever	glove	million	ocean	potato

Match Spellings & Meanings 우리말 뜻이 암기될 때까지 단어를 빈칸에 반복해서 쓰세요.

🎤 731	**promise**	▷		약속; 약속하다
🎤 732	**move**	▷		움직이다
🎤 733	**also**	▷		또한
🎤 734	**boss**	▷		(직장의) 상사, 사장
🎤 735	**bottom**	▷		바닥
🎤 736	**forever**	▷		영원히
🎤 737	**glove**	▷		장갑
🎤 738	**million**	▷		100만
🎤 739	**ocean**	▷		바다
🎤 740	**potato**	▷		감자

🔊 **Link to Sounds!** 다음 단어의 발음에 주의하여 빈칸에 들어갈 철자를 쓰세요.

pr____mise   m____ve   b____ss   b____tt____m   gl____ve   p____tat____

Voca in Stories

⭐ 몇몇 단어들은 문장에서 쓰일 때 형태나 의미가 조금 바뀌기도 해요.

731 • He **promise**d 그는 약속했다   732 • He **move**d 그는 움직였다

🖊 **Fill in the Blanks** 다음 글을 읽고 빈칸에 가장 알맞은 단어를 넣어 보세요.

1 Tom likes to visit art shows in his free time. He _____ likes to draw. He wants to be an artist.

2 How many zeros are here? There are six zeros. It's called a _____ .

3 Dolphins live in the _____ . They are smart, cute, and friendly. Many people like them.

4 I was very sick this morning. My mom called her _____ and said, "My son is very sick today. May I come late today?"

5  John loves _____ es. He likes French Fries with ketchup. 감자튀김 That is his favorite.

6 The children are playing outside in the snow. They are wearing _____ s.

7 Kevin lied to his mom again. His mom is very angry now. Kevin says, "I'm so sorry, Mom. I won't lie again. I _____ ."

8 The policeman said, "Don't _____ !" The man stopped and said, "It was not me. I didn't do anything!"

9 Kate and Mary are best friends. "We will be friends _____ !" Mary says to her mother.

10 There is a small hole in the _____ of my backpack. I need to get a new one.

Voca Itself

🔊 **Match Spellings & Sounds** 녹음을 듣고 따라 말해보세요.

poor	balloon	blood	boot	check
cook	goodbye	moon	roof	wood

Match Spellings & Meanings 우리말 뜻이 암기될 때까지 단어를 빈칸에 반복해서 쓰세요.

🎤 741	**poor**	▷		가난한
🎤 742	**balloon**	▷		풍선
🎤 743	**blood**	▷		피
🎤 744	**boot**	▷		부츠, 장화
🎤 745	**check**	▷		확인하다
🎤 746	**cook**	▷		요리사; 요리하다
🎤 747	**goodbye**	▷		안녕, 안녕히 가세요 [계세요]
🎤 748	**moon**	▷		달
🎤 749	**roof**	▷		지붕
🎤 750	**wood**	▷		나무, 목재

🔊 **Link to Sounds!** 다음 단어의 발음에 주의하여 빈칸에 들어갈 철자를 쓰세요.

ball___n   bl___d   b___t   c___k   g___dbye   m___n   r___f

Voca in Stories

⭐ 몇몇 단어들은 문장에서 쓰일 때 형태나 의미가 조금 바뀌기도 해요.

745 •He is **check**ing 그는 확인하고 있다   746 •He **cook**ed 그는 요리했다

✏ Fill in the Blanks 다음 글을 읽고 빈칸에 가장 알맞은 단어를 넣어 보세요.

1
"When will I see you
again?" Tom asked.
"I will see you next
year. _____,
Tom," said his uncle.

2
Teacher, I need five
more minutes.
I am _____
my answers now.

3

Look up there! There is a man on
the _____. What is he doing?
Oh, he is fixing the _____!

4
"Mom, I need a pair of _____s
for rainy days. My socks get wet
in the rain," said Judy.

5

The shape of the _____
changes every night in the sky.
What shape will it be tonight?

6
There are _____s at the party.
They are very pretty.

7
Mr. Kim is a very nice person. He helps
_____ children. He gives them food and
clothes for free.
무료로

8
Kate is crying on the ground.
There is _____ on her knees.
"It will be okay," says Tim.
무릎

9
Jason and his dad
are camping.
캠핑하고 있다
"Let's get more
_____. We
need to build a fire."

10
Kevin wants to be
a _____ in the
future. He likes to
_____ food for
his friends.

701~750 Review

초등코치 천일문 VOCA&STORY 2

Test Yourself! 다음 우리말을 뜻하는 영어 단어를 빈칸에 쓰고 아래 표에서 정답을 확인하세요.

701 ~ 710 ▷

1	오후	_. _.
2	메모, 쪽지	n _ _ _
3	상표, 브랜드	_ _ _ _ d
4	소풍	p _ _ _ _ _
5	~조차	e _ _ _
6	타다	r _ _ _
7	~의 위에	o _ _ _
8	누군가	a _ _ _ _ _
9	지나가다, 통과하다	_ _ _ s
10	나이가 ~인, 나이가 많은	_ _ _

/10

711 ~ 720 ▷

1	재미있는, 흥미로운	i _ _ _ _ _ _ _ _ _ _
2	~을 따라	a _ _ _ _ _
3	결혼(식)	w _ _ _ _ _ _
4	노래하다	_ _ _ _
5	저녁	e _ _ _ _ _ _
6	날개	_ _ _ _
7	반지	_ _ _ g
8	왕	_ _ _ _
9	땅, 육지	l _ _ _
10	걸다, 매달다	h _ _ _

/10

721 ~ 730 ▷

1	모래	_ _ _ _
2	멋진, 잘생긴	h _ _ _ _ _ _ _
3	친절한, 다정한	f _ _ _ _ _ _ _
4	삼각형	t _ _ _ _ _ _ _
5	서 있다	_ _ _ _ _
6	식물	_ _ _ _ _
7	땅, 땅바닥	g _ _ _ _ _
8	소리; ~하게 들리다	_ _ _ _ d
9	원숭이	_ _ _ _ _ _
10	남편	h _ _ _ _ _ _

/10

1	100만	_ _ _ _ _ _ _
2	약속; 약속하다	_ _ _ _ _ _ e
3	또한	a _ _ _
4	영원히	_ _ _ _ _ _ r
5	바다	o _ _ _ _

6	감자	_ _ _ _ _ _
7	(직장의) 상사, 사장	b _ _ _
8	움직이다	m _ _ _
9	바닥	b _ _ _ _ _
10	장갑	g _ _ _ _

/10

1	확인하다	c _ _ _ _
2	지붕	_ _ _ _
3	풍선	_ _ _ _ _ _ _
4	안녕, 안녕히 가세요[계세요]	g _ _ _ _ _ _
5	부츠, 장화	_ _ _ t

6	나무, 목재	w _ _ _
7	가난한	p _ _ _
8	피	_ _ _ _ _
9	달	_ _ _ _
10	요리사; 요리하다	c _ _ _

/10

701~750 Review | 정답

701~710	711~720	721~730	731~740	741~750
1 P.M.[p.m.]	1 interesting	1 sand	1 million	1 check
2 note	2 along	2 handsome	2 promise	2 roof
3 brand	3 wedding	3 friendly	3 also	3 balloon
4 picnic	4 sing	4 triangle	4 forever	4 goodbye
5 even	5 evening	5 stand	5 ocean	5 boot
6 ride	6 wing	6 plant	6 potato	6 wood
7 over	7 ring	7 ground	7 boss	7 poor
8 anyone	8 king	8 sound	8 move	8 blood
9 pass	9 land	9 monkey	9 bottom	9 moon
10 old	10 hang	10 husband	10 glove	10 cook

Voca Itself

🎙 **Match Spellings & Sounds** 녹음을 듣고 따라 말해보세요.

nervous	proud	could	country	couple
round	soup	sour	touch	tour

Match Spellings & Meanings 우리말 뜻이 암기될 때까지 단어를 빈칸에 반복해서 쓰세요.

🎙 751	**nervous**	▷		긴장한
🎙 752	**proud**	▷		자랑스러운
🎙 753	**could**	▷		~할 수 있었다
🎙 754	**country**	▷		시골; 나라
🎙 755	**couple**	▷		커플, 부부
🎙 756	**round**	▷		둥근
🎙 757	**soup**	▷		수프
🎙 758	**sour**	▷		(맛이) 신
🎙 759	**touch**	▷		~을 만지다
🎙 760	**tour**	▷		여행; 관광

🔊 **Link to Sounds!** 다음 단어의 발음에 주의하여 빈칸에 들어갈 철자를 쓰세요.

pr___d   c___ntry   c___ple   r___nd   s___p   t___ch

Voca in Stories

정답과 해설 p.11

⭐ 몇몇 단어들은 문장에서 쓰일 때 형태나 의미가 조금 바뀌기도 해요.

759 • He **touch**es 그는 만진다
• He **touch**ed 그는 만졌다

Fill in the Blanks 다음 글을 읽고 빈칸에 가장 알맞은 단어를 넣어 보세요.

1 My grandpa moved
<u>이사했다</u>
to the _____ .
He lived in the city
before. Now he loves
it there.

2 She skates so well!
<u>스케이트를 타다</u>
She _____ skate
even when she was
little. She will become
a great skater.

3 Look at Jake and Jenny! They
are holding hands! Are they a
_____ ? I didn't know that.

4 Don't be so _____ . You practiced hard
for this. You will do fine. We are all here for
you. Good luck!

5  Jane is sick today. Her mom made
some warm _____ for her.

6 Don't _____ that bowl yet. I put some
hot water in it. So, you need to wear gloves.

7 Do you know Kevin? He is a
tall kid in class 4. He has a
_____ face and big eyes.

8 Our _____ of China was really
great. I loved the food there. I want
to visit there again.

9 "This juice is so
_____ !" said
Tom. "Sorry, maybe I
put too much lemon
in it," said his mom.

10 I studied very hard.
So, I got a good
grade on the exam.
I am very _____ .

Voca Itself

🎧 **Match Spellings & Sounds** 녹음을 듣고 따라 말해보세요.

or	wet	case	error	record
report	store	track	uncle	work

Match Spellings & Meanings 우리말 뜻이 암기될 때까지 단어를 빈칸에 반복해서 쓰세요.

🎤 761	**or**	▷	아니면, 또는
🎤 762	**wet**	▷	젖은
🎤 763	**case**	▷	상자, 통
🎤 764	**error**	▷	잘못, 실수
🎤 765	**record**	▷	녹음하다, 녹화하다
🎤 766	**report**	▷	보도하다
🎤 767	**store**	▷	상점, 가게
🎤 768	**track**	▷	(기차) 선로; 경주로, 트랙
🎤 769	**uncle**	▷	삼촌, 외삼촌, 고모부, 이모부
🎤 770	**work**	▷	일하다

🎧 **Link to Sounds!** 다음 단어의 발음에 주의하여 빈칸에 들어갈 철자를 쓰세요.

err____   rec___d   rep___t   st___e   w___k

Voca in Stories

정답과 해설 p.11

⭐ 몇몇 단어들은 문장에서 쓰일 때 형태나 의미가 조금 바뀌기도 해요.

765 • She **record**s 그녀는 **녹음한다**   766 • She is **report**ing 그녀는 **보도하고 있다**

• Fill in the Blanks 다음 글을 읽고 빈칸에 가장 알맞은 단어를 넣어 보세요.

1 Cathy loves books. So, she wants to _____ at a library in the future.

2 My mother has a younger brother. He often visits my family. He is the best _____ in the world.

3  You can make a voice memo with your smartphone. Just press the button and _____ your voice.
누르다

4 My mother keeps her rings in her jewelry _____. She doesn't want to lose them.
보석

5 The woman on TV is _____ the news. But she is not smiling. Is everything okay?

6 I made five _____ s on the last test. And I made only two on this test. That is not bad.

7 My grandmother lives near a train station. At her house, I can hear the sound of the brakes on the _____ s.
역

8 Mary washed her shoes. But they are still _____. She can't wear them.

9 Jake, are you busy now? Can you go to the _____ next to the bakery? I need some meat.

10 Do you want the red one _____ the blue one? You can only choose one.

Voca Itself

🎙️ **Match Spellings & Sounds** 녹음을 듣고 따라 말해보세요.

own	how	follow	show	cow
crowd	down	low	slow	tower

Match Spellings & Meanings 우리말 뜻이 암기될 때까지 단어를 빈칸에 반복해서 쓰세요.

🎙️ 771	**own**	▷		자기 자신의
🎙️ 772	**how**	▷		어떻게; 얼마나
🎙️ 773	**follow**	▷		따라가다, 따라오다
🎙️ 774	**show**	▷		보여 주다
🎙️ 775	**cow**	▷		소
🎙️ 776	**crowd**	▷		군중; 대중
🎙️ 777	**down**	▷		아래로
🎙️ 778	**low**	▷		낮은
🎙️ 779	**slow**	▷		느린
🎙️ 780	**tower**	▷		탑

🎙️ **Link to Sounds!** 다음 단어의 발음에 주의하여 빈칸에 들어갈 철자를 쓰세요.

___n　h___　sh___　c___　d___n　l___　sl___

Voca in Stories

★ 몇몇 단어들은 문장에서 쓰일 때 형태나 의미가 조금 바뀌기도 해요.

773 •He **follow**ed 그는 따라갔다

Fill in the Blanks 다음 글을 읽고 빈칸에 가장 알맞은 단어를 넣어 보세요.

1 The turtle and rabbit
거북이
had a race. The
turtle was _____.
The rabbit was sure
about winning.

2 _____ do you go
to school? I go to
school by bike.
My friend Jane walks
to school.

3 Jenny looked _____ at the
floor. She found a pencil next to
her right foot. Whose is it?

4 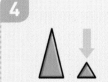 The chair is too _____ for me.
Are there any higher chairs
here?

5 Look! There is a large _____ at the
gate. What are they doing there? What are
they looking at?

6 _____s live on farms. They give
us milk and meat.

7 Sam is a new student. "Come, I will take you
to the new class," said the teacher.
So, he _____ her.

8 We climbed to the top of the
_____. It was very hard.
But the view was wonderful.

9 "Why is this the
answer?" John
asked. "Alright.
I will _____
you. Look here," said
Mary.

10 Tom has his
_____ room.
He likes to spend
time alone there.

Voca Itself

🔊 **Match Spellings & Sounds** 녹음을 듣고 따라 말해보세요.

happen	complain	spider	cup	group
helicopter	palace	spoon	supper	tape

Match Spellings & Meanings 우리말 뜻이 암기될 때까지 단어를 빈칸에 반복해서 쓰세요.

🎤 781	**happen**	▷		발생하다, 일어나다
🎤 782	**complain**	▷		불평하다
🎤 783	**spider**	▷		거미
🎤 784	**cup**	▷		컵, 잔
🎤 785	**group**	▷		그룹, 무리, 집단
🎤 786	**helicopter**	▷		헬리콥터
🎤 787	**palace**	▷		궁전
🎤 788	**spoon**	▷		숟가락, 스푼
🎤 789	**supper**	▷		저녁 식사
🎤 790	**tape**	▷		테이프

🎧 **Link to Sounds!** 다음 단어의 발음에 주의하여 빈칸에 들어갈 철자를 쓰세요.

s＿＿＿ider   cu＿＿＿   grou＿＿＿   helico＿＿＿ter   s＿＿＿oon   ta＿＿＿e

Voca in Stories

정답과 해설 p.12

⭐ 몇몇 단어들은 문장에서 쓰일 때 형태나 의미가 조금 바뀌기도 해요.

781 • It **happen**ed 그것은 일어났다   **782** • He is **complain**ing 그는 불평하고 있다

Fill in the Blanks 다음 글을 읽고 빈칸에 가장 알맞은 단어를 넣어 보세요.

1 The teacher says, "Get into a _____ of three. You cannot do it alone. You will need help from each other."

2 John, drink water in a _____. Never drink it from the bottle. Everyone drinks that water together.

3 Jake is having soup. But he drops his _____ on the floor. He needs another one.

4 Jane visits a _____ in London. There are guards at the gate. Who lives there?
경비 요원

5 There are small bugs on the web. 거미줄
Oh, they are food for a _____.

6 I want to put this picture on the wall. I need some _____.

7 Look up there! There is a _____ in the sky. Where is it going? I want to fly in it. It would be exciting!

8 "What _____ to your face?" said Kevin's mom. "Tom kicked a ball at my face. I am okay now. Don't worry," said Kevin.

9 Jim is _____ about the cold weather. "It is very cold today. I don't want to go outside."

10 My mother didn't want to cook. So, my family had pizza for _____ tonight. It was really good.

Voca Itself

🎈 **Match Spellings & Sounds** 녹음을 듣고 따라 말해보세요.

reason	glasses	possible	close	cost
desert	scientist	scissors	smell	sometimes

Match Spellings & Meanings 우리말 뜻이 암기될 때까지 단어를 빈칸에 반복해서 쓰세요.

🎤 791	**reason**	▷		이유
🎤 792	**glasses**	▷		안경
🎤 793	**possible**	▷		가능한
🎤 794	**close**	▷		닫다
🎤 795	**cost**	▷		(값·비용이) ~이다; 값, 비용
🎤 796	**desert**	▷		사막
🎤 797	**scientist**	▷		과학자
🎤 798	**scissors**	▷		가위
🎤 799	**smell**	▷		냄새를 맡다; 냄새가 나다
🎤 800	**sometimes**	▷		때때로

🎧 **Link to Sounds!** 다음 단어의 발음에 주의하여 빈칸에 들어갈 철자를 쓰세요.

rea＿＿＿on　　clo＿＿＿e　　co＿＿＿t　　＿＿＿mell　　＿＿＿ometime＿＿＿

Voca in Stories

정답과 해설 p.13

⭐ 몇몇 단어들은 문장에서 쓰일 때 형태나 의미가 조금 바뀌기도 해요.

795 • It **costs** 그것은 (값·비용이) ~이다

● Fill in the Blanks 다음 글을 읽고 빈칸에 가장 알맞은 단어를 넣어 보세요.

1 Jenny didn't come to school today. Do you know the _____? Is she sick? Did she go <u>somewhere</u>?
어딘가에

2 My family likes to eat at home, but _____ we go out for dinner. We do it once a week.

3 <u>Camels</u> save water in their bodies.
낙타
So, they can live in dry places. They are _____ animals.

4 Jason likes science class. He likes to read science books. He wants to be a _____ in the future.

5 Mike wears _____. But when he plays basketball, he takes them off. He doesn't want to break them.

6 Sam, this computer _____ a lot. We don't have enough money for it. Let's look around some more.

7 Can you _____ the door behind you? It's cold. Wind is coming through the door.

8 Do you have _____? I need to cut this in smaller pieces.

9 "Mom, do you _____ that? Something <u>is burning</u>," said Amy.
타고 있다
"Oh, no! My cookies!"

10 Pigs cannot fly. It is not _____. They don't have wings. Plus, they are really heavy.

751~800 Review

ON OFF

✏ **Test Yourself!** 다음 우리말을 뜻하는 영어 단어를 빈칸에 쓰고 아래 표에서 정답을 확인하세요.

751 ~ 760 ▷

1	자랑스러운	_ _ _ _ _
2	시골; 나라	c _ _ _ _ _ _
3	여행; 관광	t _ _ _
4	긴장한	n _ _ _ _ _ _
5	~할 수 있었다	c _ _ _ _

6	둥근	_ _ _ _ _
7	커플, 부부	_ _ _ _ _ _
8	~을 만지다	_ _ _ _ _
9	수프	_ _ _ _
10	(맛이) 신	s _ _ _

/10

761 ~ 770 ▷

1	젖은	_ _ _
2	보도하다	r _ _ _ _ _
3	(기차) 선로; 경주로, 트랙	_ _ _ _ _
4	일하다	_ _ _ _
5	상점, 가게	s _ _ _ _

6	잘못, 실수	e _ _ _ _
7	녹음하다, 녹화하다	r _ _ _ _ _
8	삼촌, 외삼촌, 고모부, 이모부	_ _ _ _ _
9	아니면, 또는	o _
10	상자, 통	c _ _ _

/10

771 ~ 780 ▷

1	탑	t _ _ _ _ _
2	아래로	d _ _ _
3	느린	_ _ _ _
4	자기 자신의	o _ _
5	따라가다, 따라오다	_ _ _ _ _ _

6	군중; 대중	c _ _ _ _
7	소	_ _ _
8	낮은	_ _ _
9	보여 주다	s _ _ _
10	어떻게; 얼마나	_ _ _

/10

781 ~ 790 ▷

1	숟가락, 스푼	_ _ _ _ _
2	불평하다	c _ _ _ _ _ _ _
3	거미	_ _ _ _ _ _
4	저녁 식사	s _ _ _ _ _
5	궁전	_ _ _ _ _ _

6	테이프	_ _ _ _
7	발생하다, 일어나다	h _ _ _ _ _
8	헬리콥터	_ _ _ _ _ _ _ _ _ _
9	그룹, 무리, 집단	_ _ _ _ _
10	컵, 잔	_ _ _

/10

791 ~ 800 ▷

1	사막	_ _ _ _ _ _
2	이유	r _ _ _ _ _ _
3	때때로	_ _ _ _ _ _ _ _ _
4	(값·비용이) ~ 이다; 값, 비용	c _ _ _
5	가위	_ _ _ _ _ _ _ _

6	과학자	_ _ _ _ _ _ _ _ _
7	닫다	c _ _ _ _
8	가능한	p _ _ _ _ _ _
9	냄새를 맡다; 냄새가 나다	_ _ _ _ _
10	안경	g _ _ _ _ _ _

/10

751~800 Review | 정답

751~760	761~770	771~780	781~790	791~800
1 proud	1 wet	1 tower	1 spoon	1 desert
2 country	2 report	2 down	2 complain	2 reason
3 tour	3 track	3 slow	3 spider	3 sometimes
4 nervous	4 work	4 own	4 supper	4 cost
5 could	5 store	5 follow	5 palace	5 scissors
6 round	6 error	6 crowd	6 tape	6 scientist
7 couple	7 record	7 cow	7 happen	7 close
8 touch	8 uncle	8 low	8 helicopter	8 possible
9 soup	9 or	9 show	9 group	9 smell
10 sour	10 case	10 how	10 cup	10 glasses

Voca Itself

🔊 **Match Spellings & Sounds** 녹음을 듣고 따라 말해보세요.

shout	hope	cash	fish	fresh
however	large	leaf	shape	shop

Match Spellings & Meanings 우리말 뜻이 암기될 때까지 단어를 빈칸에 반복해서 쓰세요.

🎤 801	**shout**	▷	소리치다, 소리 지르다
🎤 802	**hope**	▷	희망; 바라다
🎤 803	**cash**	▷	현금, 돈
🎤 804	**fish**	▷	물고기
🎤 805	**fresh**	▷	신선한
🎤 806	**however**	▷	하지만, 그러나
🎤 807	**large**	▷	큰
🎤 808	**leaf**	▷	나뭇잎
🎤 809	**shape**	▷	모양
🎤 810	**shop**	▷	가게, 상점

🔊 **Link to Sounds!** 다음 단어의 발음에 주의하여 빈칸에 들어갈 철자를 쓰세요.

____out   ca____   fi____   fre____   ____ape   ____op

Voca in Stories

정답과 해설 p.13

⭐ 몇몇 단어들은 문장에서 쓰일 때 형태나 의미가 조금 바뀌기도 해요.

801 ・He **shout**ed 그는 소리쳤다

802 ・She **hope**s 그녀는 바란다

✏️ **Fill in the Blanks** 다음 글을 읽고 빈칸에 가장 알맞은 단어를 넣어 보세요.

1 Jenny likes to bake cookies. She makes them in different _____s, like a circle, a star, and a heart.

2 Susan _____ to visit the city again. She really liked everything about it.

3 My mother doesn't use _____. She only uses her card. She doesn't like to carry a lot of _____.

4 Jason saw Kate across the street. He _____ to her. "Kate! Where are you going?"

5 "Did you catch any _____?" Ben asked. "Shh. You will scare them <u>away</u>," said his dad.
쫓아버리다

6 "There is a _____ on your head. Did you sit under a tree?" asked John. "Yes. Please take it off," said Mary.

7 There are five people in my family. So, we always buy a _____ pizza. But sometimes it is not enough.

8 There is a new mall in the town. They have many _____s, a movie theater, and many restaurants, too.

9 Mike's parents love nature. They often visit parks and forests. They love the trees and the _____ air.

10 Jenny needs a new bag. _____, she doesn't have enough money.

Voca Itself

🎙 **Match Spellings & Sounds** 녹음을 듣고 따라 말해보세요.

discuss	focus	fool	glad	skin
sky	step	stick	stone	stress

Match Spellings & Meanings 우리말 뜻이 암기될 때까지 단어를 빈칸에 반복해서 쓰세요.

🎙 811	**discuss**	▷		논의하다, 토론하다
🎙 812	**focus**	▷		집중하다
🎙 813	**fool**	▷		바보
🎙 814	**glad**	▷		기쁜, 반가운
🎙 815	**skin**	▷		피부
🎙 816	**sky**	▷		하늘
🎙 817	**step**	▷		(발)걸음
🎙 818	**stick**	▷		막대기
🎙 819	**stone**	▷		돌
🎙 820	**stress**	▷		스트레스

🔊 **Link to Sounds!** 다음 단어의 발음에 주의하여 빈칸에 들어갈 철자를 쓰세요.

____in ____y ____ep ____ick ____one ____ress

Voca in Stories

정답과 해설 p.13

⭐ 몇몇 단어들은 문장에서 쓰일 때 형태나 의미가 조금 바뀌기도 해요.

811 • They are **discuss**ing 그들은 논의하고 있다

Fill in the Blanks 다음 글을 읽고 빈칸에 가장 알맞은 단어를 넣어 보세요.

1 There is a big sports event tomorrow. The students are _____ the plans for the event.

2 Too much sun is not good for your _____. Wear a cap outside on sunny days.

3 The donkey falls into the river. Now the
당나귀
bag is heavier. "You _____, they were sponges, not salt," said the man.

4 Jake, take one _____ back from there. You should stand behind this line.

5 Tim likes to look up into the night _____. He can see the stars and the moon.

6 Jane slipped on a _____ and
~에 미끄러졌다
fell. She got dirty. She needs to be more careful!

7 Mom, can you turn the TV volume down? I can't _____. I have to study for a test.

8 It was getting cold at the campsite.
캠프장
"Let's find some _____s. We have to make a fire," said Tom.

9 My dad gets too much _____ from work. He can't sleep well. He needs a break.

10 I am so _____ to see you in this class. We will have so much fun this year.

821~830 words

Voca Itself

🔊 **Match Spellings & Sounds** 녹음을 듣고 따라 말해보세요.

beauty	congratulate	countryside	culture	cut
flat	pants	past	tiger	toward

Match Spellings & Meanings 우리말 뜻이 암기될 때까지 단어를 빈칸에 반복해서 쓰세요.

🎤 821	**beauty**	▶		아름다움, 미
🎤 822	**congratulate**	▶		축하하다
🎤 823	**countryside**	▶		시골 지역
🎤 824	**culture**	▶		문화
🎤 825	**cut**	▶		자르다
🎤 826	**flat**	▶		평평한
🎤 827	**pants**	▶		바지
🎤 828	**past**	▶		과거
🎤 829	**tiger**	▶		호랑이
🎤 830	**toward**	▶		～을 향하여

🔊 **Link to Sounds!** 다음 단어의 발음에 주의하여 빈칸에 들어갈 철자를 쓰세요.

congra____ulate　　coun____ryside　　cul____ure

Voca **in Stories**

정답과 해설 **p.14**

★ 몇몇 단어들은 문장에서 쓰일 때 형태나 의미가 조금 바뀌기도 해요.

822 •They **congratulated** 그들은 축하했다   **825** •He **cut**s 그는 자른다

Fill in the Blanks 다음 글을 읽고 빈칸에 가장 알맞은 단어를 넣어 보세요.

1 Today, we ride in cars. We can also fly on a plane. But people in the _____ rode horses.

2 Ben's family traveled through the _____. They saw farms and fields. They had a great time.

3 Kate fell down this morning. She is okay. But now there is a small hole in her _____.

4 Most _____s have yellow or orange <u>fur</u>. They are big and wild. But the babies are cute.
털

5 The cat is walking _____ the woman. She is holding some cat food and water. "Come on, kitty," she says.

6 The man finally arrives on the top of the mountain. He enjoys the great view. He loves the _____ of nature.

7 The <u>barber</u> _____ Tom's hair.
이발사
It is too short now. Tom doesn't like it.

8 Jake <u>won first prize</u> at a contest.
1등을 했다
His family and friends _____ him.

9 Most countries have their own _____s. We learned about them in class today. It was interesting.

10 My mother made pizza. She put it on a large _____ <u>plate</u>. I ate three
접시
pieces!

Voca Itself

🎧 **Match Spellings & Sounds** 녹음을 듣고 따라 말해보세요.

bath	cloth	death	hit	introduce
nothing	other	than	thin	thousand

Match Spellings & Meanings 우리말 뜻이 암기될 때까지 단어를 빈칸에 반복해서 쓰세요.

🎤 831	**bath**	▶		목욕
🎤 832	**cloth**	▶		천
🎤 833	**death**	▶		죽음
🎤 834	**hit**	▶		때리다, 치다
🎤 835	**introduce**	▶		소개하다
🎤 836	**nothing**	▶		아무것도 (~아니다[없다])
🎤 837	**other**	▶		다른, 그 밖의
🎤 838	**than**	▶		~보다
🎤 839	**thin**	▶		얇은, 가는
🎤 840	**thousand**	▶		1000, 천

🔊 **Link to Sounds!** 다음 단어의 발음에 주의하여 빈칸에 들어갈 철자를 쓰세요.

ba____   clo____   dea____   no____ing   o____er   ____an   ____in

Voca **in Stories**

정답과 해설 **p.14**

⭐ 몇몇 단어들은 문장에서 쓰일 때 형태나 의미가 조금 바뀌기도 해요.

834 • He **hit** 그는 **때렸다**   835 • She **introduce**d 그녀는 **소개했다**

(**Fill in the Blanks**) 다음 글을 읽고 빈칸에 가장 알맞은 단어를 넣어 보세요.

1
Jenny is taller
_____ Mary.
So, Jenny sits behind
Mary in class.

2
Cathy went on a trip
to China last year.
Now she wants to
visit _____
countries. Where will
she go?

3
Ben's mother wanted to change
the curtains. She bought some
_____ and made new ones.

4
Mike is sad. His pet died last week.
The _____ came so <u>suddenly</u>.
갑자기

5

"Is someone in the bathroom?" Hans
asked. "Mom is taking a _____,"
his brother answered.

6
You cannot skate there. The ice is
very _____ . You will fall into
the ice cold water.

7
Jane _____ Kate to her sister.
"This is my sister, Sara. Sara, this is Kate,"
said Jane.

8

Jake _____ his brother in the
arm. His brother started to cry.
Mom was really angry.

9
There is
_____
in the bag.
It's <u>empty</u>. Where
비어 있는
did I put my pencil
case?

10
My mom only gives
two _____
won to me every
week. It's not
enough. I need more.

Voca Itself

🎧 **Match Spellings & Sounds** 녹음을 듣고 따라 말해보세요.

popular	careful	truth	business	button
duck	glue	produce	puppy	send

Match Spellings & Meanings 우리말 뜻이 암기될 때까지 단어를 빈칸에 반복해서 쓰세요.

🎤 841	**popular**	▷		인기 있는
🎤 842	**careful**	▷		조심하는, 주의 깊은
🎤 843	**truth**	▷		사실
🎤 844	**business**	▷		(직장의) 일, 업무
🎤 845	**button**	▷		단추; 버튼
🎤 846	**duck**	▷		오리
🎤 847	**glue**	▷		풀, 접착제
🎤 848	**produce**	▷		생산하다
🎤 849	**puppy**	▷		강아지
🎤 850	**send**	▷		보내다

🔊 **Link to Sounds!** 다음 단어의 발음에 주의하여 빈칸에 들어갈 철자를 쓰세요.

pop____lar   caref___l   tr___th   b____tton   d___ck   prod____ce

Voca in Stories

정답과 해설 p.14

⭐ 몇몇 단어들은 문장에서 쓰일 때 형태나 의미가 조금 바뀌기도 해요.

848 ·It **produce**s 그것은 생산한다

Fill in the Blanks 다음 글을 읽고 빈칸에 가장 알맞은 단어를 넣어 보세요.

1 My dad is in China. He is away on _____ . I miss him.

2 The factory in my town _____ computers. It makes lots of them each month.

3 Sam will _____ a birthday card to his friend Mark. "Mark will be very surprised," Sam said.

4 A _____ came off my jacket. But I don't see it on the floor. Where is it?

5 I need to stick this homework list
붙이다
on my notebook. Do you have _____ ?

6 Kate got a _____ from her grandmother. "It's so cute. Let's call her Molly," said Kate.

7 Mom, I will tell the _____ . I didn't go to the piano lesson today. I played with my friends instead. I am so sorry.

8 A mommy _____ is making sounds in the water. Quack! Quack! Oh, she is calling her babies.

9 That boy is very _____ . He is good at sports. And he is nice to everyone. All the girls like him.

10 Do you need scissors? Here you are. Be _____ . They are very sharp.

801~850 Review

Test Yourself! 다음 우리말을 뜻하는 영어 단어를 빈칸에 쓰고 아래 표에서 정답을 확인하세요.

801 ~ 810 ▷

1	하지만, 그러나	_ _ _ _ _ _ _
2	큰	l _ _ _ _ _
3	현금, 돈	c _ _ _
4	소리치다, 소리 지르다	_ _ _ _ _
5	나뭇잎	l _ _ _
6	물고기	_ _ _ _
7	가게, 상점	s _ _ _
8	신선한	_ _ _ _ _
9	모양	s _ _ _ _
10	희망; 바라다	_ _ _ _

/10

811 ~ 820 ▷

1	집중하다	f _ _ _ _
2	피부	_ _ _ _
3	스트레스	_ _ _ _ _ _
4	논의하다, 토론하다	d _ _ _ _ _ _
5	바보	_ _ _ _
6	기쁜, 반가운	g _ _ _
7	돌	_ _ _ _ _
8	하늘	_ _ _
9	막대기	s _ _ _ _
10	(발)걸음	s _ _ _

/10

821 ~ 830 ▷

1	시골 지역	c _ _ _ _ _ _ _ _ _ _ _
2	축하하다	c _ _ _ _ _ _ _ _ _ _ _
3	~을 향하여	t _ _ _ _ _ _
4	자르다	c _ _
5	평평한	_ _ _ _
6	문화	_ _ _ _ _ _ _
7	바지	p _ _ _ _
8	호랑이	_ _ _ _ _
9	과거	_ _ _ _
10	아름다움, 미	_ _ _ _ _ _

/10

831 ~ 840 ▷

1	죽음	_ _ _ _ _
2	소개하다	_ _ _ _ _ _ _ _ _
3	1000, 천	_ _ _ _ _ _ _ _
4	때리다, 치다	h _ _
5	아무것도 (~아니다[없다])	n _ _ _ _ _ _

6	천	c _ _ _ _
7	목욕	_ _ _ _
8	~보다	_ _ _ _
9	얇은, 가는	t _ _ _
10	다른, 그 밖의	o _ _ _ _

/10

841 ~ 850 ▷

1	단추; 버튼	_ _ _ _ _ _
2	오리	_ _ _ _
3	생산하다	p _ _ _ _ _ _
4	(직장의) 일, 업무	b _ _ _ _ _ _ _
5	조심하는, 주의 깊은	c _ _ _ _ _ _

6	보내다	_ _ _ _
7	강아지	p _ _ _ _
8	인기 있는	_ _ _ _ _ _ _
9	풀, 접착제	_ _ _ _
10	사실	t _ _ _ _

/10

801~850 Review | 정답

801~810	811~820	821~830	831~840	841~850
1 however	1 focus	1 countryside	1 death	1 button
2 large	2 skin	2 congratulate	2 introduce	2 duck
3 cash	3 stress	3 toward	3 thousand	3 produce
4 shout	4 discuss	4 cut	4 hit	4 business
5 leaf	5 fool	5 flat	5 nothing	5 careful
6 fish	6 glad	6 culture	6 cloth	6 send
7 shop	7 stone	7 pants	7 bath	7 puppy
8 fresh	8 sky	8 tiger	8 than	8 popular
9 shape	9 stick	9 past	9 thin	9 glue
10 hope	10 step	10 beauty	10 other	10 truth

Voca Itself

🎧 **Match Spellings & Sounds** 녹음을 듣고 따라 말해보세요.

save	leave	both	camera	fire
hill	if	level	river	violin

✏️ **Match Spellings & Meanings** 우리말 뜻이 암기될 때까지 단어를 빈칸에 반복해서 쓰세요.

🎤 851	**save**	▷	구하다; 저축하다
🎤 852	**leave**	▷	떠나다, 출발하다
🎤 853	**both**	▷	둘 다; 양쪽의
🎤 854	**camera**	▷	카메라
🎤 855	**fire**	▷	불, 화재
🎤 856	**hill**	▷	언덕
🎤 857	**if**	▷	만약 ~라면
🎤 858	**level**	▷	정도; 수준
🎤 859	**river**	▷	강
🎤 860	**violin**	▷	바이올린

🔊 **Link to Sounds!** 다음 단어의 발음에 주의하여 빈칸에 들어갈 철자를 쓰세요.

sa___e   lea___e   le___el   ri___er   ___iolin

Voca in Stories

⭐ 몇몇 단어들은 문장에서 쓰일 때 형태나 의미가 조금 바뀌기도 해요.

851 •He **save**s 그는 구한다   852 •It left 그것은 떠났다

Fill in the Blanks 다음 글을 읽고 빈칸에 가장 알맞은 단어를 넣어 보세요.

1 My family sometimes go to this _____. We go fishing and take boats. But we can't swim here. It's too deep.

2 The _____ of this book is very high. There are many difficult words in it.

3 Tom ran to the bus stop. But the bus already _____ the bus stop. Tom has to wait for another one.

4 He rides in a red truck. He puts out _____s. He saves people. What is his job?
끄다

5 I can't decide between vanilla and chocolate ice cream. But I don't have enough money for _____.

6 I play the _____. My brother plays the piano. My mom sings along with our music.

7 A boy fell into the pool. "Help me!" said the boy. "I will _____ you." The lifeguard jumped into the pool.
안전 요원

8 My dad's phone has a _____. He takes pictures and videos with it.

9 The kids climbed to the top of the _____. It was hard, but they loved the view from the _____.

10 _____ it's warm tomorrow, we will go out. Where do you want to go?

Voca Itself

🎙 **Match Spellings & Sounds** 녹음을 듣고 따라 말해보세요.

worried	wake	write	drawing	newspaper
power	town	twice	wide	wife

✏ **Match Spellings & Meanings** 우리말 뜻이 암기될 때까지 단어를 빈칸에 반복해서 쓰세요.

🎙 861	**worried**	▷	걱정하는
🎙 862	**wake**	▷	잠에서 깨다, 일어나다
🎙 863	**write**	▷	쓰다
🎙 864	**drawing**	▷	그림
🎙 865	**newspaper**	▷	신문
🎙 866	**power**	▷	힘
🎙 867	**town**	▷	(소)도시
🎙 868	**twice**	▷	두 번
🎙 869	**wide**	▷	넓은, 폭이 넓은
🎙 870	**wife**	▷	아내, 부인

🎧 **Link to Sounds!** 다음 단어의 발음에 주의하여 빈칸에 들어갈 철자를 쓰세요.

____orried   ____ake   dra____ing   po____er   t____ice   ____ife

Voca in Stories

정답과 해설 **p.15**

⭐ 몇몇 단어들은 문장에서 쓰일 때 형태나 의미가 조금 바뀌기도 해요.

862 • He woke 그는 잠에서 깼다

Fill in the Blanks 다음 글을 읽고 빈칸에 가장 알맞은 단어를 넣어 보세요.

1 My dad writes a letter for my mom. "Happy birthday! You are the best _____ for me. I love you."

2 Ben bought a new bed. But it is too _____. He cannot get it through the door!

3  Do you have a pen? I need to _____ something down. Can I borrow one?

4 When John _____ up, it was already 9 o'clock. He was very late for school. So, he had to stay after class.

5 The man in the movie had great _____. He could lift anything. 들어 올리다 I want to be strong, too.

6 Jane called Tom _____. But he didn't answer the phone. Did something happen to him?

7 My dad is reading a _____ now. "Honey, it will rain tomorrow. Don't forget your umbrella!"

8 "Tom, you came home late. I was _____ about you," his mom said. "Sorry, Mom. I played soccer outside," Tom said.

9 The teacher looked at the kids' _____ s. "You all did very great! They are all beautiful."

10 Dad got a new car. So, he drove with us around the _____. I like the new car!

Voca Itself

🔊 **Match Spellings & Sounds** 녹음을 듣고 따라 말해보세요.

put	shower	allowance	wonder	bench
hero	pig	police	which	worker

Match Spellings & Meanings 우리말 뜻이 암기될 때까지 단어를 빈칸에 반복해서 쓰세요.

🎤 871	**put**	▷		놓다, 두다
🎤 872	**shower**	▷		샤워(하기)
🎤 873	**allowance**	▷		용돈
🎤 874	**wonder**	▷		궁금하다
🎤 875	**bench**	▷		벤치
🎤 876	**hero**	▷		영웅
🎤 877	**pig**	▷		돼지
🎤 878	**police**	▷		경찰
🎤 879	**which**	▷		어느, 어떤
🎤 880	**worker**	▷		노동자, 근로자

🔊 **Link to Sounds!** 다음 단어의 발음에 주의하여 빈칸에 들어갈 철자를 쓰세요.

sho____er　　allo____ance　　____onder　　____orker

Voca in Stories

정답과 해설 p.16

⭐ 몇몇 단어들은 문장에서 쓰일 때 형태나 의미가 조금 바뀌기도 해요.

871 •She put 그녀는 **놓았다**

874 •She **wondered** 그녀는 궁금했다

📝 **Fill in the Blanks** 다음 글을 읽고 빈칸에 가장 알맞은 단어를 넣어 보세요.

1 " _____ color do you like better, yellow or orange?" asked Tim. "I like orange," said Jake.

2 "Mom, where did you _____ my jeans?" asked Tom. "They're in the drawer." said his mom.
서랍

3 There is a small _____ right under the tree. We can sit over there and take a break.

4 There are many _____s at the factory. They start to work at 9 a.m. and finish at 5 p.m.

5  Jason played soccer all day. He sweated a lot. He needs a _____ .
땀을 흘렸다

6 Oink! Oink! What is that sound? Oh, there is a _____ in the mud. I didn't see him there.
진흙

7 'How did he know that?' she _____ . She wanted to ask him. But he left already.

8  Amy found a wallet on the street. She took it to the _____ . They will find the owner.
주인

9 I get an _____ every week from my parents. It is not a lot. But I save it in my piggy bank.
저금통

10 There was a big fire in town. But firemen came and saved everyone. They are brave _____ es.

Voca Itself

🟦 **Match Spellings & Sounds** 녹음을 듣고 따라 말해보세요.

excited	example	experience	express	fox
lion	middle	print	taxi	textbook

Match Spellings & Meanings 우리말 뜻이 암기될 때까지 단어를 빈칸에 반복해서 쓰세요.

🎤 881	**excited**	▷		신이 난, 흥분한
🎤 882	**example**	▷		예, 보기
🎤 883	**experience**	▷		경험
🎤 884	**express**	▷		표현하다
🎤 885	**fox**	▷		여우
🎤 886	**lion**	▷		사자
🎤 887	**middle**	▷		중앙, 가운데
🎤 888	**print**	▷		인쇄하다, 프린트하다
🎤 889	**taxi**	▷		택시
🎤 890	**textbook**	▷		교과서

🔊 **Link to Sounds!** 다음 단어의 발음에 주의하여 빈칸에 들어갈 철자를 쓰세요.

e____cited　　e____ample　　e____perience　　e____press　　fo____　　ta____i

Voca in Stories

정답과 해설 p.16

⭐ 몇몇 단어들은 문장에서 쓰일 때 형태나 의미가 조금 바뀌기도 해요.

888 • She is **print**ing 그녀는 인쇄하고 있다

🔍 Fill in the Blanks 다음 글을 읽고 빈칸에 가장 알맞은 단어를 넣어 보세요.

1
Babies can't speak.
But they _____
their feelings. They
cry when they are
hungry or sleepy.

2
Red is an _____
of a color. Seven is
an _____ of a
number.

3
What animal has red <u>fur</u>, a big tail,
            털
and big ears? You are right.
It is a _____ !

4
Kate is _____ something
for her homework. But <u>suddenly</u>
                        갑자기
the printer stops! That is no good!

5

Ben is sitting on my right side.
Jake is sitting on my left side.
I am in the _____ of them.

6
I just got my new _____ for
next year. Wow, it looks interesting. But it
looks a little hard, too.

7
Tom draws an animal. It is big and
has long hair around its face.
Oh, it is a _____ !

8

My father is late for work. He doesn't
have enough time to take a bus.
So, he calls a _____ .

9
The children are
_____ . They will
visit the <u>amusement</u>
          놀이공원
<u>park</u> tomorrow.
It is their first time.

10
My trip to China was
a great _____ !
I did a lot of things.
I won't forget it.

Voca Itself

🔊 **Match Spellings & Sounds** 녹음을 듣고 따라 말해보세요.

cry	cycle	elementary	fry	history
honey	marry	money	slowly	type

Match Spellings & Meanings 우리말 뜻이 암기될 때까지 단어를 빈칸에 반복해서 쓰세요.

🎤 891	**cry**	▷		울다
🎤 892	**cycle**	▷		순환
🎤 893	**elementary**	▷		초등학교의
🎤 894	**fry**	▷		(기름에) 굽다, 튀기다
🎤 895	**history**	▷		역사
🎤 896	**honey**	▷		꿀
🎤 897	**marry**	▷		결혼하다
🎤 898	**money**	▷		돈
🎤 899	**slowly**	▷		천천히
🎤 900	**type**	▷		유형, 종류

🔊 **Link to Sounds!** 다음 단어의 발음에 주의하여 빈칸에 들어갈 철자를 쓰세요.

cr____   elementar____   fr____   histor____   marr____   t____pe

Voca in Stories

⭐ 몇몇 단어들은 문장에서 쓰일 때 형태나 의미가 조금 바뀌기도 해요.

891 •He is **cry**ing 그는 울고 있다   894 •She is **fry**ing 그녀는 (기름에) 튀기고 있다

Fill in the Blanks 다음 글을 읽고 빈칸에 가장 알맞은 단어를 넣어 보세요.

1 Ben is in school now. But after a few years, he will be in middle school.

2 My class visited a museum. We saw many interesting old things. We learned about the _____ of Korea.

3 "Will you _____ me?" said the prince. The princess said yes to his proposal.
프로포즈, 청혼

4  Mike wants to be rich. He wants to make a lot of _____. He wants to help poor people.

5 My mom always adds _____ instead of sugar in juice. It tastes the same.

6 The baby is _____. He just woke up. Maybe he is hungry. Where is his mom?

7 The seasons come in a _____: spring, summer, fall, winter, and then spring again.

8 Mike's mother is _____ chicken for dinner. It smells really good in here. Mike is really hungry now.
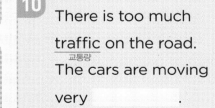

9 That _____ of dog has long flat ears and short legs. It looks different from other dogs.

10 There is too much traffic on the road.
교통량
The cars are moving very _____.

851~900 Review

Test Yourself! 다음 우리말을 뜻하는 영어 단어를 빈칸에 쓰고 아래 표에서 정답을 확인하세요.

851 ~ 860 ▷

1	바이올린	v _ _ _ _ _	6	언덕	h _ _ _
2	둘 다; 양쪽의	b _ _ _	7	강	_ _ _ _ _
3	만약 ~라면	_ _	8	떠나다, 출발하다	_ _ _ _ e
4	정도; 수준	l _ _ _ _	9	카메라	_ _ _ _ _ _
5	불, 화재	_ _ _ _	10	구하다; 저축하다	s _ _ _

/10

861 ~ 870 ▷

1	신문	n _ _ _ _ _ _ _ _	6	(소)도시	t _ _ _
2	아내, 부인	_ _ _ _	7	힘	p _ _ _ _
3	두 번	_ _ _ _ e	8	걱정하는	_ _ _ _ _ _ _
4	그림	d _ _ _ _ _ _	9	잠에서 깨다, 일어나다	w _ _ _
5	쓰다	_ _ _ _ _	10	넓은, 폭이 넓은	_ _ _ _

/10

871 ~ 880 ▷

1	영웅	h _ _ _	6	놓다, 두다	_ _ _
2	샤워(하기)	s _ _ _ _ _	7	어느, 어떤	w _ _ _ _
3	벤치	_ _ _ _ _	8	노동자, 근로자	_ _ _ _ _ _
4	경찰	p _ _ _ _ _	9	용돈	a _ _ _ _ _ _ _ _
5	돼지	_ _ _	10	궁금하다	_ _ _ _ _ r

/10

881 ~ 890 ▷

1	경험	e _ _ _ _ _ _ _ _ _
2	중앙, 가운데	m _ _ _ _ _
3	택시	_ _ _ _
4	신이 난, 흥분한	_ _ _ _ _ _ d
5	표현하다	_ _ _ _ _ _ _
6	여우	_ _ _
7	예, 보기	_ _ _ _ _ _ e
8	사자	_ _ _ _
9	교과서	t _ _ _ _ _ _ _
10	인쇄하다, 프린트하다	p _ _ _ _

/10

891 ~ 900 ▷

1	(기름에) 굽다, 튀기다	f _ _
2	순환	_ _ _ _ e
3	초등학교의	e _ _ _ _ _ _ _ _ _
4	역사	_ _ _ _ _ _ _
5	천천히	s _ _ _ _ _
6	돈	m _ _ _ _
7	유형, 종류	t _ _ _
8	꿀	h _ _ _ _
9	울다	_ _ _
10	결혼하다	_ _ _ _ _

/10

851~900 Review | 정답

851~860	861~870	871~880	881~890	891~900
1 violin	1 newspaper	1 hero	1 experience	1 fry
2 both	2 wife	2 shower	2 middle	2 cycle
3 if	3 twice	3 bench	3 taxi	3 elementary
4 level	4 drawing	4 police	4 excited	4 history
5 fire	5 write	5 pig	5 express	5 slowly
6 hill	6 town	6 put	6 fox	6 money
7 river	7 power	7 which	7 example	7 type
8 leave	8 worried	8 worker	8 lion	8 honey
9 camera	9 wake	9 allowance	9 textbook	9 cry
10 save	10 wide	10 wonder	10 print	10 marry

901~910 words

Voca Itself

🎙 **Match Spellings & Sounds** 녹음을 듣고 따라 말해보세요.

mean	amazing	jam	joy	mall
puzzle	size	turn	zebra	zoo

Match Spellings & Meanings 우리말 뜻이 암기될 때까지 단어를 빈칸에 반복해서 쓰세요.

🎙 901	**mean**	▷		의미하다
🎙 902	**amazing**	▷		놀랄 만한, 굉장한
🎙 903	**jam**	▷		잼
🎙 904	**joy**	▷		기쁨, 즐거움
🎙 905	**mall**	▷		쇼핑몰
🎙 906	**puzzle**	▷		퍼즐, 수수께끼
🎙 907	**size**	▷		크기, 치수
🎙 908	**turn**	▷		돌다, 꺾다
🎙 909	**zebra**	▷		얼룩말
🎙 910	**zoo**	▷		동물원

🔊 **Link to Sounds!** 다음 단어의 발음에 주의하여 빈칸에 들어갈 철자를 쓰세요.

ama____ing   si____e   ____ebra   ____oo

Voca in Stories

정답과 해설 p.17

⭐ 몇몇 단어들은 문장에서 쓰일 때 형태나 의미가 조금 바뀌기도 해요.

901 • It **mean**s 그것은 의미한다

(`Fill in the Blanks`) 다음 글을 읽고 빈칸에 가장 알맞은 단어를 넣어 보세요.

1 When you shake your head, it usually 보통 _____ "no."

2 Do you see the green building over there? _____ right at the corner.

3  This _____ is very big. Let's take a look at the map. I want to see the giraffes first.

4 I like the color of this shirt, but it is too big for me. The arms are too long. Do you have a smaller _____?

5 I put strawberry _____ on my toast. My brother likes apple _____ on his toast.

6 My sister played the piano well at the contest. It was _____! She won first prize. 1등을 했다 I am very proud of her.

7 _____s are different from horses. They have black and white stripes on their body. 줄무늬

8 Ben and Jake are doing _____s. "Where should I put this piece?" asked Jake.

9 Jane and Mike are in the _____. Eric's birthday is coming. So, they need to buy a present for him.

10 My mother met her best friend from elementary school. She cried for _____.

Voca Itself

🔊 **Match Spellings & Sounds** 녹음을 듣고 따라 말해보세요.

rule	run	guess	guitar	guy
language	quick	quite	up	usually

Match Spellings & Meanings 우리말 뜻이 암기될 때까지 단어를 빈칸에 반복해서 쓰세요.

🎤 911	**rule**	▷		규칙
🎤 912	**run**	▷		달리다, 뛰다
🎤 913	**guess**	▷		추측하다
🎤 914	**guitar**	▷		기타
🎤 915	**guy**	▷		남자
🎤 916	**language**	▷		언어
🎤 917	**quick**	▷		빠른
🎤 918	**quite**	▷		꽤, 아주
🎤 919	**up**	▷		위로
🎤 920	**usually**	▷		보통, 평소에는

🎧 **Link to Sounds!** 다음 단어의 발음에 주의하여 빈칸에 들어갈 철자를 쓰세요.

r____le   r____n   g____y   lang____age   ____p   ____s____ally

Voca in Stories

⭐ 몇몇 단어들은 문장에서 쓰일 때 형태나 의미가 조금 바뀌기도 해요.

912 • He is **run**ning 그는 달리고 있다

Fill in the Blanks 다음 글을 읽고 빈칸에 가장 알맞은 단어를 넣어 보세요.

1 Uncle Jack is a nice _____. He is very kind to everyone. He is very handsome, too.

2 "You did _____ well on the test. You got 90 points. Well done, Jason," said the teacher.

3 Tom can play the piano. Now he wants to play the _____. He wants to join the school band.

4 There are a few _____s here in the class. First, you cannot eat during the class. It is very rude.
예의 없는

5 "This elevator is going _____," said the man. "Oh, I'll wait for the next one. I'm going down," I said.

6 Jane speaks two _____s, Korean and English. But she wants to learn another one, too.

7 Sam is _____ to the station. The train will leave in 5 minutes. Run faster, Sam!

8 "Teacher, I am done!" said Mary. "That was _____," said the teacher.

9 Kate _____ waits for her sister at the gate. But today it was very cold. She didn't wait for her.

10 I have many holes. I can hold water. What am I? Can you _____? I am a sponge!

Voca Itself

🎧 **Match Spellings & Sounds** 녹음을 듣고 따라 말해보세요.

grade	comfortable	card	dry	interest
mark	part	rabbit	serve	yard

Match Spellings & Meanings 우리말 뜻이 암기될 때까지 단어를 빈칸에 반복해서 쓰세요.

🎤	921	**grade**	▷		학년; 성적
🎤	922	**comfortable**	▷		편안한
🎤	923	**card**	▷		카드
🎤	924	**dry**	▷		마른, 건조한
🎤	925	**interest**	▷		관심, 흥미
🎤	926	**mark**	▷		표시
🎤	927	**part**	▷		일부; 부분
🎤	928	**rabbit**	▷		토끼
🎤	929	**serve**	▷		제공하다
🎤	930	**yard**	▷		마당

🎧 **Link to Sounds!** 다음 단어의 발음에 주의하여 빈칸에 들어갈 철자를 쓰세요.

g＿＿ade　　d＿＿y　　inte＿＿＿est　　ma＿＿k　　pa＿＿t　　＿＿abbit

Voca in Stories

⭐ 몇몇 단어들은 문장에서 쓰일 때 형태나 의미가 조금 바뀌기도 해요.

929 • It **serve**s 그것은 제공한다

Fill in the Blanks 다음 글을 읽고 빈칸에 가장 알맞은 단어를 넣어 보세요.

1 The sixth _____ went to the museum yesterday. Today, the fifth _____ will visit the farm.

2 I loved the <u>ending</u> 결말 of the story. What about you? Which _____ was your favorite?

3 Look at those long ears and the short tail. That _____ is so cute. It is hopping on the grass.
깡충깡충 뛰고 있다

4 Mom, this chair is not very _____. It is too high for me. I can't touch the floor with my feet. I need another one.

5 There is a small _____ on my desk. It is not my birthday. Who is this from?

6 What is this black _____ on the map? I should ask my dad. He might know something.

7 My mom wants to have a house with a _____. She wants to plant flowers there.

8 This restaurant _____ a great lunch menu. The price is good, too. Let's go there.

9 I have a small toy in my hand. My dog looks at it. He shows _____. Maybe he wants to play.

10 Jenny, those socks are not _____ yet. You should <u>put on</u> 입다 other ones.

Voca Itself

🔵 **Match Spellings & Sounds** 녹음을 듣고 따라 말해보세요.

rest	secret	pet	lady	prince
prize	process	radio	soft	spread

Match Spellings & Meanings 우리말 뜻이 암기될 때까지 단어를 빈칸에 반복해서 쓰세요.

🎤 931	**rest**	▷		휴식; 쉬다
🎤 932	**secret**	▷		비밀
🎤 933	**pet**	▷		애완동물
🎤 934	**lady**	▷		여자 분, 여성
🎤 935	**prince**	▷		왕자
🎤 936	**prize**	▷		상
🎤 937	**process**	▷		과정
🎤 938	**radio**	▷		라디오
🎤 939	**soft**	▷		부드러운
🎤 940	**spread**	▷		펴다, 펼치다

🔵 **Link to Sounds!** 다음 단어의 발음에 주의하여 빈칸에 들어갈 철자를 쓰세요.

____ince   ____ize   ____ocess   s____ead

Voca in Stories

⭐ 몇몇 단어들은 문장에서 쓰일 때 형태나 의미가 조금 바뀌기도 해요.

931 •They are **rest**ing 그들은 쉬고 있다   940 •He spread 그는 폈다

🖊 **Fill in the Blanks** 다음 글을 읽고 빈칸에 가장 알맞은 단어를 넣어 보세요.

1 The _____ finds a glass shoe. "Wait! Don't go! What is your name?" But Cinderella 신데렐라 doesn't look back.

2 When you clean your glasses, you should always use a _____ cloth. Don't use anything else!

3 I really want to have a _____. But my mother is scared of small animals.

4 The _____ of making ice cream is really easy. Mix cream and sugar together. Then put it in the freezer. 냉동실

5 The teacher _____ the map on the desk. "Look, there is a small island right here. Does anyone know the name of it?"

6 Mike's drawing won a _____. What did he draw? He drew his family. Good job, Mike!

7 Who is that _____ over there? She said hi to me. Oh, that's Jake's mother.

8 Kevin's father listens to the _____ in his car. He likes to listen to the music and the news.

9 The kids played soccer for too long. They need a break. They are _____ under a tree.

10 Did you hear this? Ben likes Jenny. Don't tell anybody. It is a _____.

Voca Itself

🔵 **Match Spellings & Sounds** 녹음을 듣고 따라 말해보세요.

feed	more	helpful	hint	mouse
out	plane	sale	salt	sofa

Match Spellings & Meanings 우리말 뜻이 암기될 때까지 단어를 빈칸에 반복해서 쓰세요.

🎤 941	**feed**	▷		먹이를 주다
🎤 942	**more**	▷		더 많은
🎤 943	**helpful**	▷		도움이 되는
🎤 944	**hint**	▷		힌트, 단서
🎤 945	**mouse**	▷		쥐
🎤 946	**out**	▷		밖에, 밖으로
🎤 947	**plane**	▷		비행기
🎤 948	**sale**	▷		세일, 할인 판매
🎤 949	**salt**	▷		소금
🎤 950	**sofa**	▷		소파

🎧 **Link to Sounds!** 다음 단어의 발음에 주의하여 빈칸에 들어갈 철자를 쓰세요.

pl___ne   s___le   s___lt   sof___

Voca in Stories

정답과 해설 p.18

⭐ 몇몇 단어들은 문장에서 쓰일 때 형태나 의미가 조금 바뀌기도 해요.

941 ·He **feed**s 그는 먹이를 준다

Fill in the Blanks 다음 글을 읽고 빈칸에 가장 알맞은 단어를 넣어 보세요.

1 "Dad, here it is," Mary said. "Thanks, Mary. You were _____," her dad said.

2 Can you _____ the dog for me? I am late for my swimming lesson. I will _____ him tomorrow.

3 "It wasn't sugar!" Mom put _____ in her coffee by mistake. 실수로 She can't drink it now.

4 "Hello, may I speak to John, please?" Tom said. "Sorry, he is not here. John just went _____," said John's mom.

5 Jason's family is sitting on the _____. They are watching a baseball game on TV together.

6 My cat is running around the house. He is following something. What is 따라가고 있다 that? Oh! That is a _____!

7 Jake is waiting for his dad at the airport. "Mom! The _____ will arrive soon!"

8 There is a big _____ at the mall this weekend. My parents hope to get things at good prices. I'll go with them, too.

9 Can you give me a _____? I still don't know the answer to the question.

10 Dave wants to get a cap. It is ten dollars, but he has only six dollars. He needs _____ money.

901~950 Review

Test Yourself! 다음 우리말을 뜻하는 영어 단어를 빈칸에 쓰고 아래 표에서 정답을 확인하세요.

901 ~ 910 ▷

1	잼	_ _ _
2	의미하다	m _ _ _
3	동물원	_ _ _
4	얼룩말	_ e _ _ _
5	퍼즐, 수수께끼	_ u _ _ _ _

6	놀랄 만한, 굉장한	a _ _ _ _ _ _
7	크기, 치수	s _ _ _
8	쇼핑몰	_ _ _ _
9	기쁨, 즐거움	_ _ y
10	돌다, 꺾다	_ _ r _

/10

911 ~ 920 ▷

1	기타	_ _ i _ _ _
2	보통, 평소에는	_ _ u _ _ _ _
3	위로	_ p
4	규칙	r _ _ _
5	꽤, 아주	q _ _ _ _

6	추측하다	_ _ e _ _
7	달리다, 뛰다	_ _ _
8	빠른	q _ _ _ _
9	언어	_ _ _ _ _ _ _ e
10	남자	_ u _

/10

921 ~ 930 ▷

1	토끼	_ _ _ _ _ _
2	카드	_ _ _ _
3	표시	_ a _ _
4	마당	_ _ _ d
5	학년; 성적	g _ _ _ _

6	일부; 부분	_ _ r _
7	관심, 흥미	i _ _ _ _ _ _ _
8	편안한	_ _ _ f _ _ _ _ _ _ _
9	제공하다	_ _ _ _ e
10	마른, 건조한	d _ _

/10

931 ~ 940 ▷

1	휴식; 쉬다	_ _ _ t	6	상	p _ _ _ _
2	왕자	_ _ _ _ _ _	7	라디오	_ _ _ _ _
3	애완동물	_ _ _	8	부드러운	_ _ f _
4	펴다, 펼치다	_ p _ _ _ _	9	과정	_ _ _ _ e _ _
5	여자 분, 여성	_ _ d _	10	비밀	s _ _ _ _ _

/10

941 ~ 950 ▷

1	소파	s _ _ _	6	힌트, 단서	_ _ _ t
2	소금	_ _ _ _	7	더 많은	_ _ r _
3	먹이를 주다	_ _ _ _	8	세일, 할인 판매	_ _ _ _
4	비행기	_ l _ _ _	9	밖에, 밖으로	_ u _
5	쥐	_ _ u _ _	10	도움이 되는	_ _ _ _ _ _ _

/10

901~950 Review | 정답

901~910	911~920	921~930	931~940	941~950
1 jam	1 guitar	1 rabbit	1 rest	1 sofa
2 mean	2 usually	2 card	2 prince	2 salt
3 zoo	3 up	3 mark	3 pet	3 feed
4 zebra	4 rule	4 yard	4 spread	4 plane
5 puzzle	5 quite	5 grade	5 lady	5 mouse
6 amazing	6 guess	6 part	6 prize	6 hint
7 size	7 run	7 interest	7 radio	7 more
8 mall	8 quick	8 comfortable	8 soft	8 sale
9 joy	9 language	9 serve	9 process	9 out
10 turn	10 guy	10 dry	10 secret	10 helpful

Voca Itself

🎧 **Match Spellings & Sounds** 녹음을 듣고 따라 말해보세요.

scary	decision	direction	either	jacket
necessary	result	sell	sentence	silent

Match Spellings & Meanings 우리말 뜻이 암기될 때까지 단어를 빈칸에 반복해서 쓰세요.

🎤 951	**scary**	▷		무서운
🎤 952	**decision**	▷		결정
🎤 953	**direction**	▷		방향
🎤 954	**either**	▷		(둘 중) 어느 하나(의)
🎤 955	**jacket**	▷		재킷
🎤 956	**necessary**	▷		필요한
🎤 957	**result**	▷		결과
🎤 958	**sell**	▷		팔다
🎤 959	**sentence**	▷		문장
🎤 960	**silent**	▷		조용한

🔊 **Link to Sounds!** 다음 단어의 발음에 주의하여 빈칸에 들어갈 철자를 쓰세요.

d___cision   dir___ction   jack___t   r___sult   s___ll

Voca in Stories

⭐ 몇몇 단어들은 문장에서 쓰일 때 형태나 의미가 조금 바뀌기도 해요.

958 ・He **sell**s 그는 판다
・She **sold** 그녀는 팔았다

🔖 **Fill in the Blanks** 다음 글을 읽고 빈칸에 가장 알맞은 단어를 넣어 보세요.

1 When you write a question, you have to put a <u>question mark</u>
물음표
at the end of the
_____ .

2 Kate loves
_____ movies.
She likes the ones with ghosts. But her friends don't like them much.

3 Dad, there is a new shop near our house. They _____ and fix bikes there.

4  You may choose _____ the pie or the cake. But you can't have both.

5 I came home after school. There was no one at home. The house was _____ .

6 Don't forget to put on your _____ . It is windy out there. You will be very cold without it.

7 "Now, I will tell you the _____ of the contest. Guess who is the <u>winner</u>!" said the
우승자
teacher.

8 "Are we going in the right _____ ?" asked Mary. "I will check the map again," said Tim.

9 Kate needs to make a _____ .
Will she go to Jake's birthday party or Tom's?

10 I need to bring paints and a sketchbook to school. They are _____
for art class.

Voca Itself

🎧 **Match Spellings & Sounds** 녹음을 듣고 따라 말해보세요.

terrible	spicy	let	prepare	side
simple	star	ticket	tiny	trade

Match Spellings & Meanings 우리말 뜻이 암기될 때까지 단어를 빈칸에 반복해서 쓰세요.

🎤 961	**terrible**	▷		끔찍한
🎤 962	**spicy**	▷		매운
🎤 963	**let**	▷		~하게 하다
🎤 964	**prepare**	▷		준비하다
🎤 965	**side**	▷		쪽, 옆, 면
🎤 966	**simple**	▷		간단한
🎤 967	**star**	▷		별
🎤 968	**ticket**	▷		표, 티켓
🎤 969	**tiny**	▷		아주 작은
🎤 970	**trade**	▷		거래, 무역

🔵 **Link to Sounds!** 다음 단어의 발음에 주의하여 빈칸에 들어갈 철자를 쓰세요.

terr____ble　　sp____cy　　s____de　　s____mple　　t____cket　　t____ny

Voca in Stories

★ 몇몇 단어들은 문장에서 쓰일 때 형태나 의미가 조금 바뀌기도 해요.

963 • She **let** 그녀는 ~하게 했다

964 • They are **prepar**ing 그들은 준비하고 있다

Fill in the Blanks 다음 글을 읽고 빈칸에 가장 알맞은 단어를 넣어 보세요.

1 There will be a _____ storm tomorrow. Kids have no school. They have to stay inside.

2 The test was very easy and _____. I finished it really quickly.

3 This puppy is so _____. I can hold him in one hand. Look at those small paws! They are cute.
동물의 발

4 We can't see any _____s tonight. It is so cloudy. Maybe tomorrow, we will have clear sky.

5 On the right _____, you will see a bank. The <u>bookstore</u> is next to the bank.
서점
What book will you buy there?

6 Mary is eating pizza. How is it, Mary? Oh, she drinks a lot of water. It must be very _____.
~임이 틀림없다

7 "Show your _____, please," said the man. "Okay. Here you are," said Jake. "Enjoy the movie!"

8 Korea does a lot of _____ with China. These two countries buy and sell many things.

9 Jane is helping her mother in the kitchen. They are _____ dinner.

10 I want to go out now. But it is too dark outside. My mom won't _____ me go.

Voca Itself

🎈 **Match Spellings & Sounds** 녹음을 듣고 따라 말해보세요.

clothes	once	lose	among	government
hole	hot	most	rope	song

Match Spellings & Meanings 우리말 뜻이 암기될 때까지 단어를 빈칸에 반복해서 쓰세요.

🎤 971	**clothes**	▷	옷, 의복
🎤 972	**once**	▷	한 번
🎤 973	**lose**	▷	잃어버리다; 지다
🎤 974	**among**	▷	~의 사이에(서)
🎤 975	**government**	▷	정부
🎤 976	**hole**	▷	구멍
🎤 977	**hot**	▷	매운
🎤 978	**most**	▷	대부분, 대부분의; 가장
🎤 979	**rope**	▷	밧줄
🎤 980	**song**	▷	노래

🎧 **Link to Sounds!** 다음 단어의 발음에 주의하여 빈칸에 들어갈 철자를 쓰세요.

cl___thes   ___nce   l___se   h___le   h___t   m___st

Voca in Stories

⭐ 몇몇 단어들은 문장에서 쓰일 때 형태나 의미가 조금 바뀌기도 해요.

973 •She lost 그녀는 잃어버렸다

🔵 **Fill in the Blanks** 다음 글을 읽고 빈칸에 가장 알맞은 단어를 넣어 보세요.

1 There is a house _____ the trees. I didn't know that. That house is hiding in the tall trees.

2 A nation has a _____ . It works for the people in the country. It tries to make a better country.

3 Mom came home from work. My dad and I started to sing a birthday _____ for her.

4 Ben visits his uncle _____ a month. Ben wants to go there every week, but he can't.

5 Mom, this soup is too _____ for me. I need some water.

6 There was a _____ in my sock. So, I had to take it off and put on a new one.

7 Jake fell into a deep well. He can't 우물 climb back up again. "Here, grab this _____ !" said the man.

8 Kate _____ her book in the classroom. "Where did I put it? I can't remember!"

9 Jane's mom says, "The weather will get cold soon. We need to get our winter _____ out."

10 _____ children like amusement 놀이공원 parks. Many families go there on Children's Day.

Voca Itself

🎧 **Match Spellings & Sounds** 녹음을 듣고 따라 말해보세요.

huge	upset	theater	spend	skate
hug	coat	race	tent	until

Match Spellings & Meanings 우리말 뜻이 암기될 때까지 단어를 빈칸에 반복해서 쓰세요.

🎤 981	**huge**	▷	거대한
🎤 982	**upset**	▷	속상한, 마음이 상한
🎤 983	**theater**	▷	극장
🎤 984	**spend**	▷	(돈을) 쓰다; (시간을) 보내다
🎤 985	**skate**	▷	스케이트를 타다
🎤 986	**hug**	▷	포옹
🎤 987	**coat**	▷	외투, 코트
🎤 988	**race**	▷	경주
🎤 989	**tent**	▷	텐트, 천막
🎤 990	**until**	▷	~까지

🎧 **Link to Sounds!** 다음 단어의 발음에 주의하여 빈칸에 들어갈 철자를 쓰세요.

h____ge   ____pset   h____g   ____ntil

Voca in Stories

정답과 해설 p.20

⭐ 몇몇 단어들은 문장에서 쓰일 때 형태나 의미가 조금 바뀌기도 해요.

984 • He spent 그는 썼다

985 • She **skate**s 그녀는 스케이트를 탄다

Fill in the Blanks 다음 글을 읽고 빈칸에 가장 알맞은 단어를 넣어 보세요.

1 Nate _____ all his money on snacks. Now, he doesn't have any money.

2 John, you can play computer games _____ 7 o'clock. After that, you can't play more.

3 Jenny's favorite season is winter. She loves winter sports. She often _____ at the ice rink.
스케이트장

4 Mary's dad is putting up a _____. "Mary, can you bring the hammer?" asked her dad.
망치

5 Jenny's brother dropped her smartphone on the floor. After that, sound didn't come out. Jenny was so _____.

6 The prince lives in a _____ castle. There are so many rooms. Sometimes he can't find his.

7 My _____ is very old. It is not warm anymore. I need a new _____.

8 I gave some flowers to my mother. She was very surprised. "Thank you," she said. Then she gave me a _____.
그리고 나서

9 My brother is crying. He came in last in the _____. It's okay, brother. You did good!

10 Hans is waiting for Jason at the _____. The movie will start soon. But Jason is late. Hurry up, Jason!

Voca Itself

🎧 **Match Spellings & Sounds** 녹음을 듣고 따라 말해보세요.

noodle	pair	share	pool	cool

joke	wave	action	hamburger	noon	page

Match Spellings & Meanings 우리말 뜻이 암기될 때까지 단어를 빈칸에 반복해서 쓰세요.

🎤 991	**noodle**	▷		국수
🎤 992	**pair**	▷		(두 개로 된) 한 쌍[켤레, 벌]
🎤 993	**share**	▷		함께 쓰다, 공유하다
🎤 994	**pool**	▷		수영장
🎤 995	**cool**	▷		멋진
🎤 996	**joke**	▷		농담
🎤 997	**wave**	▷		파도
🎤 998	**action**	▷		행동
🎤 999	**hamburger**	▷		햄버거
🎤 1000	**noon**	▷		정오, 낮 12시
🎤 1001	**page**	▷		페이지, 쪽

Voca in Stories

★ 몇몇 단어들은 문장에서 쓰일 때 형태나 의미가 조금 바뀌기도 해요.

993 •They are **shar**ing 그들은 함께 쓰고 있다

Fill in the Blanks 다음 글을 읽고 빈칸에 가장 알맞은 단어를 넣어 보세요.

1 Your phone is really _____. Can I see it? Do you have any games on it?

2 Teacher, I need help with this. I don't understand the problem on _____ 11.

3 Ben has many _____s of socks. He has them in many different colors.

4  It is _____. It's almost lunchtime. What is today's lunch menu?

5 Jenny went to the _____. But too many people were swimming there. She had to wait.

6 Kate doesn't have an umbrella. Jane has one. So, they are _____ Jane's umbrella.

7  I don't want to have _____s for dinner. I want rice instead.

8 Ben wanted to have a _____. But his mom said, "That's not healthy."

9 Hans, that was just a _____. Don't be mad. I didn't want to hurt you.
감정을 상하게 하다

10 The sea is very calm today. The children are playing in the _____s.

11 A doctor's quick _____ saves many lives. One minute is very important.

951~1001 Review ⓞⓝ ⓞⓕⓕ

🖊 **Test Yourself!** 다음 우리말을 뜻하는 영어 단어를 빈칸에 쓰고 아래 표에서 정답을 확인하세요.

951 ~ 960 ▷

1	결과	r _ _ _ _ _ _
2	조용한	s _ _ _ _ _
3	재킷	_ _ _ _ e _
4	팔다	_ _ _ _
5	결정	d _ _ _ _ _ _ _

6	(둘 중) 어느 하나(의)	_ i _ _ _ _
7	문장	_ _ _ _ _ _ _ _
8	무서운	s _ _ _ _
9	필요한	_ e _ _ _ _ _ _
10	방향	_ _ _ _ _ _ _ _ n

/10

961 ~ 970 ▷

1	거래, 무역	_ _ _ _ e
2	아주 작은	_ _ _ y
3	끔찍한	_ _ r _ _ _ _ _
4	쪽, 옆, 면	_ _ d _
5	~하게 하다	_ _ t

6	매운	_ _ i _ _
7	표, 티켓	_ _ _ _ _ _
8	간단한	_ i _ _ _ _
9	준비하다	_ _ e _ _ _ _
10	별	_ _ _ _

/10

971 ~ 980 ▷

1	대부분, 대부분의; 가장	_ o _ _
2	옷, 의복	c _ _ _ _ _ _
3	밧줄	r _ _ _
4	정부	_ _ _ _ r _ _ _ _
5	구멍	_ _ _ _

6	노래	_ _ _ _
7	잃어버리다; 지다	_ _ _ _
8	매운	_ o _
9	~의 사이에(서)	a _ _ _ _
10	한 번	_ _ c _

/10

981 ~ 990 ▷

1	거대한	_ _ g _
2	텐트, 천막	t _ _ _
3	극장	_ h _ _ _ _ _
4	포옹	h _ _
5	스케이트를 타다	_ _ _ _ _
6	(시간을) 보내다, (돈을) 쓰다	_ _ _ _ _
7	~까지	_ _ _ i _
8	경주	r _ _ _
9	속상한, 마음이 상한	_ _ _ e _
10	외투, 코트	_ _ _ _

/10

991 ~ 1001 ▷

1	파도	_ _ _ e
2	행동	_ _ _ i _ _
3	페이지, 쪽	_ _ _ _
4	(두 개로 된) 한 쌍[켤레, 벌]	_ _ i _
5	정오, 낮 12시	_ _ _ n
6	수영장	_ _ o _
7	멋진	c _ _ _
8	국수	_ _ _ _ _ _
9	햄버거	_ _ _ _ _ _ _ _ _
10	함께 쓰다, 공유하다	_ _ a _ _
11	농담	j _ _ _

/11

951~1001 Review | 정답

951~960	961~970	971~980	981~990	991~1001
1 result	1 trade	1 most	1 huge	1 wave
2 silent	2 tiny	2 clothes	2 tent	2 action
3 jacket	3 terrible	3 rope	3 theater	3 page
4 sell	4 side	4 government	4 hug	4 pair
5 decision	5 let	5 hole	5 skate	5 noon
6 either	6 spicy	6 song	6 spend	6 pool
7 sentence	7 ticket	7 lose	7 until	7 cool
8 scary	8 simple	8 hot	8 race	8 noodle
9 necessary	9 prepare	9 among	9 upset	9 hamburger
10 direction	10 star	10 once	10 coat	10 share
				11 joke

memo ✍

memo ✍

memo

EGU
THE EASIEST GRAMMAR & USAGE

EGU 시리즈 소개

EGU 서술형 기초 세우기

영단어&품사

서술형·문법의 기초가 되는
영단어와 품사 결합 학습

문장 형식

기본 동사 32개를 활용한
문장 형식별 학습

동사 써먹기

기본 동사 24개를 활용한
확장식 문장 쓰기 연습

EGU 서술형·문법 다지기

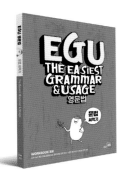

문법 써먹기

개정 교육 과정
중1 서술형·문법 완성

구문 써먹기

개정 교육 과정
중2, 중3 서술형·문법 완성

초 등 코 치

천일문
voca&story

2

· WORKBOOK ·

CEDU
BOOK

초등코치

천일문
voca&story

◆ ◆ ◆

WORKBOOK

2

⭐ 다음 각 그림과 우리말을 연결하세요. 그리고 우리말에 해당하는 영어를 빈칸에 반복해서 써보세요.

		개미	1
		(음식을) 굽다	2
		공책	3
		농구	4

⭐ 다음 각 우리말에 해당하는 영어를 빈칸에 쓰세요.

지역	5		행진하다	10	
공원	6		그녀는 굽고 있다	11	
기초	7		그는 행진하고 있다	12	
앉다	8		그녀는 앉아 있다	13	
중요한	9				

⭐ 다음 각 그림과 우리말을 연결하세요. 그리고 우리말에 해당하는 영어를 빈칸에 반복해서 써보세요.

		침실	1
		장소	2
		작은	3
		핀, 클립	4
		건너다	5

⭐ 다음 각 우리말에 해당하는 영어를 빈칸에 쓰세요.

표면	6		거의	10	
관심을 가지다, 상관하다	7		그녀는 관심을 가진다	11	
마을	8		그는 관심을 가졌다	12	
~보다 위에	9				

Master 521~530 words

정답 p.22

⭐ 다음 각 그림과 우리말을 연결하세요. 그리고 우리말에 해당하는 영어를 빈칸에 반복해서 써보세요.

페인트; 페인트를 칠하다	1	
사슬, 쇠줄	2	
다리	3	
새장; 우리	4	

⭐ 다음 각 우리말에 해당하는 영어를 빈칸에 쓰세요.

이미, 벌써	5	수영하다	9	
여행; 여행하다	6	진짜의	10	
주된, 주요한	7	그녀는 수영한다	11	
~에 반대하여 [맞서]	8			

Master 531~540 words

정답 p.22

⭐ 다음 각 그림과 우리말을 연결하세요. 그리고 우리말에 해당하는 영어를 빈칸에 반복해서 써보세요.

카트, 손수레	1	
뼈	2	
도시	3	
가지고 가다; 잡다	4	

⭐ 다음 각 우리말에 해당하는 영어를 빈칸에 쓰세요.

~때문에	5	환영하다	9	
~한 맛이 나다; 맛	6	식당, 레스토랑	10	
이모, 고모	7	그는 가지고 갔다	11	
(성인) 여자	8	그녀는 환영했다	12	

Master 541~550 words

정답 p.22

⭐ 다음 각 그림과 우리말을 연결하세요. 그리고 우리말에 해당하는 영어를 빈칸에 반복해서 써보세요.

	항공사	1
	지불하다	2
	일기	3
	지하철	4

⭐ 다음 각 우리말에 해당하는 영어를 빈칸에 쓰세요.

(음악) 밴드	5	길, 방법	9
떨어져	6	학원	10
주의 깊게	7	그녀는 놓았다	11
놓다, 두다	8	그는 지불했다	12

Master 551~560 words

정답 p.22

⭐ 다음 각 그림과 우리말을 연결하세요. 그리고 우리말에 해당하는 영어를 빈칸에 반복해서 써보세요.

	과학	1
	연필	2
	자전거	3
	복사하다	4
	옮기다	5

⭐ 다음 각 우리말에 해당하는 영어를 빈칸에 쓰세요.

졸리는	6	(얼마의 시간) ~전에	9
기회	7	거리, 도로	10
기초의, 기본적인	8	그는 옮기고 있다	11

Master 561~570 words

정답 p.22

⭐ 다음 각 그림과 우리말을 연결하세요. 그리고 우리말에 해당하는 영어를 빈칸에 반복해서 써보세요.

			초콜릿	1
떨어지다	2
기계	3

⭐ 다음 각 우리말에 해당하는 영어를 빈칸에 쓰세요.

저렴한, 값싼	4		일, 직장	9
각각의	5		끝; 끝나다	10
그러한	6		그녀는 바꾸었다	11
안녕	7		그들은 떨어지고 있다	12
바꾸다	8		그것은 끝났다	13

Master 571~580 words

정답 p.22

⭐ 다음 각 그림과 우리말을 연결하세요. 그리고 우리말에 해당하는 영어를 빈칸에 반복해서 써보세요.

			인형	1
나뭇가지	2
깃발	3

⭐ 다음 각 우리말에 해당하는 영어를 빈칸에 쓰세요.

그리다	4		모으다	8
정확한	5		영향; 효과	9
농장	6		과목	10
~옆에	7		그녀는 그렸다	11

Master 581~590 words

정답 p.22

⭐ 다음 각 그림과 우리말을 연결하세요. 그리고 우리말에 해당하는 영어를 빈칸에 반복해서 써보세요.

			배낭, 책가방	1	
			주머니	2	
			돌, 바위	3	
			양말	4	

⭐ 다음 각 우리말에 해당하는 영어를 빈칸에 쓰세요.

수표	5		구역, 블록	9
트럭	6		따다, 줍다	10
충격	7		그는 딴다	11
~처럼	8			

Master 591~600 words

정답 p.22

⭐ 다음 각 그림과 우리말을 연결하세요. 그리고 우리말에 해당하는 영어를 빈칸에 반복해서 써보세요.

			~보다 아래에	1	
			영화관	2	
			들어가다	3	

⭐ 다음 각 우리말에 해당하는 영어를 빈칸에 쓰세요.

브레이크, 제동 장치	4		완료하다; 완전한	9
엔진	5		에너지, 활기	10
대회	6		그들은 들어가고 있다	11
즐기다	7		그녀는 즐겼다	12
코미디	8			

Master 601~610 words

정답 p.22

⭐ 다음 각 그림과 우리말을 연결하세요. 그리고 우리말에 해당하는 영어를 빈칸에 반복해서 써보세요.

	치즈	1	
	나무	2	
	씨, 씨앗	3	
	벌	4	

⭐ 다음 각 우리말에 해당하는 영어를 빈칸에 쓰세요.

속도	5		동의하다	9
엔지니어, 기술자	6		(계속) 가지고 있다	10
십 대	7		그녀는 가지고 있다	11
달콤한, 단	8		그녀는 동의한다	12

Master 611~620 words

정답 p.22

⭐ 다음 각 그림과 우리말을 연결하세요. 그리고 우리말에 해당하는 영어를 빈칸에 반복해서 써보세요.

	빵	1	
	말하다	2	
	청바지	3	
	열, 뜨거움	4	
	아이스크림	5	

⭐ 다음 각 우리말에 해당하는 영어를 빈칸에 쓰세요.

인도하다, 안내하다	6		죽은	10
천국	7		그녀는 인도하고 있다	11
평화	8		그녀는 인도했다	12
대신에	9			

Master 621~630 words

정답 p.23

⭐ 다음 각 그림과 우리말을 연결하세요. 그리고 우리말에 해당하는 영어를 빈칸에 반복해서 써보세요.

농부	1	
종이	2	
화, 분노	3	
가리다, 덮다	4	
아파트	5	

⭐ 다음 각 우리말에 해당하는 영어를 빈칸에 쓰세요.

연주회, 콘서트	6		결정하다	9
구성원, 회원	7		직원, 점원	10
나중에	8		그들은 결정했다	11

Master 631~640 words

정답 p.23

⭐ 다음 각 그림과 우리말을 연결하세요. 그리고 우리말에 해당하는 영어를 빈칸에 반복해서 써보세요.

거품	1	
얼음	2	
공장	3	
백, 100	4	

⭐ 다음 각 우리말에 해당하는 영어를 빈칸에 쓰세요.

삶, 생명	5		환상적인	9
통제하다	6		잔디, 풀	10
뚱뚱한, 살찐	7		그녀는 통제한다	11
멀리, 떨어져	8			

Master 641~650 words

정답 p.23

⭐ 다음 각 그림과 우리말을 연결하세요. 그리고 우리말에 해당하는 영어를 빈칸에 반복해서 써보세요.

위험	1	
개구리	2	
신사	3	
대문, 출입문	4	
기린	5	

⭐ 다음 각 우리말에 해당하는 영어를 빈칸에 쓰세요.

대화	6		대학	10
용서하다	7		그녀는 용서했다	11
이기다; 때리다	8		그들은 이겼다	12
가수	9			

Master 651~660 words

정답 p.23

⭐ 다음 각 그림과 우리말을 연결하세요. 그리고 우리말에 해당하는 영어를 빈칸에 반복해서 써보세요.

(전깃)불, (전)등	1	
밤	2	
똑바로	3	
무게	4	

⭐ 다음 각 우리말에 해당하는 영어를 빈칸에 쓰세요.

~을 통해	5		사냥하다	9
밝은	6		용감한	10
춤을 추다; 춤	7		그는 ~일지도 모른다	11
~일지도 모른다, ~일수도 있다	8			

⭐ 다음 각 그림과 우리말을 연결하세요. 그리고 우리말에 해당하는 영어를 빈칸에 반복해서 써보세요.

	재미없는, 지루한	1
	섬	2
	병원	3
	닭; 닭고기	4

⭐ 다음 각 우리말에 해당하는 영어를 빈칸에 쓰세요.

습관	5	마침내	9
죽이다	6	~ 안으로	10
사촌	7	그는 초대한다	11
초대하다	8	그는 초대했다	12

Master 671~680 words

⭐ 다음 각 그림과 우리말을 연결하세요. 그리고 우리말에 해당하는 영어를 빈칸에 반복해서 써보세요.

	날다	1
	동그라미, 원	2
	셔츠	3
	치마	4

⭐ 다음 각 우리말에 해당하는 영어를 빈칸에 쓰세요.

잡다	5	영리한, 똑똑한	9
탄생, 출생	6	~옆에	10
갈증, 목마름	7	그는 잡는다	11
특히	8		

Master 681~690 words

정답 p.23

⭐ 다음 각 그림과 우리말을 연결하세요. 그리고 우리말에 해당하는 영어를 빈칸에 반복해서 써보세요.

○ ○ 목록, 리스트	1	
○ ○ 유리; 유리잔	2	
○ ○ 세계, 세상	3	
○ ○ 곰	4	

⭐ 다음 각 우리말에 해당하는 영어를 빈칸에 쓰세요.

축제	5		호수	9
상징	6		나누다	10
파일	7		그는 나눴다	11
야생의	8			

Master 691~700 words

정답 p.23

⭐ 다음 각 그림과 우리말을 연결하세요. 그리고 우리말에 해당하는 영어를 빈칸에 반복해서 써보세요.

○ ○ 회사	1	
○ ○ 뛰다, 점프하다	2	
○ ○ 고양이	3	
○ ○ 숲	4	

⭐ 다음 각 우리말에 해당하는 영어를 빈칸에 쓰세요.

잠깐; 순간	5		아름다운	10
손님, 고객	6		그들은 뛰고 있다	11
형태	7		그는 ~인 것처럼 보인다	12
~인 것처럼 보이다	8			
~해야 하다	9			

⭐ 다음 각 그림과 우리말을 연결하세요. 그리고 우리말에 해당하는 영어를 빈칸에 반복해서 써보세요.

누군가	1	
메모, 쪽지	2	
타다	3	
~의 위에	4	
소풍	5	

⭐ 다음 각 우리말에 해당하는 영어를 빈칸에 쓰세요.

오후	6	나이가 ~인, 나이가 많은	10	
상표, 브랜드	7	그들은 탔다	11	
지나가다, 통과하다	8	그것은 지나갔다	12	
~조차	9			

Master 711~720 words

정답 p.23

⭐ 다음 각 그림과 우리말을 연결하세요. 그리고 우리말에 해당하는 영어를 빈칸에 반복해서 써보세요.

저녁	1	
왕	2	
땅, 육지	3	
걸다, 매달다	4	
반지	5	

⭐ 다음 각 우리말에 해당하는 영어를 빈칸에 쓰세요.

~을 따라	6	노래하다	10	
결혼(식)	7	그는 건다	11	
재미있는, 흥미로운	8	그는 걸었다	12	
날개	9			

⭐ 다음 각 그림과 우리말을 연결하세요. 그리고 우리말에 해당하는 영어를 빈칸에 반복해서 써보세요.

		삼각형	1
		모래	2
		소리; ~하게 들리다	3
		땅, 땅바닥	4

⭐ 다음 각 우리말에 해당하는 영어를 빈칸에 쓰세요.

서 있다	5		원숭이	9
남편	6		멋진, 잘생긴	10
친절한, 다정한	7		그들은 서 있었다	11
식물	8			

⭐ 다음 각 그림과 우리말을 연결하세요. 그리고 우리말에 해당하는 영어를 빈칸에 반복해서 써보세요.

		감자	1
		움직이다	2
		장갑	3
		바다	4

⭐ 다음 각 우리말에 해당하는 영어를 빈칸에 쓰세요.

바닥	5		영원히	9
100만	6		또한	10
(직장의) 상사, 사장	7		그는 움직였다	11
약속; 약속하다	8		그는 약속했다	12

Master 741~750 words

정답 p.24

⭐ 다음 각 그림과 우리말을 연결하세요. 그리고 우리말에 해당하는 영어를 빈칸에 반복해서 써보세요.

	피	1
	풍선	2
	지붕	3
	달	4
	부츠, 장화	5

⭐ 다음 각 우리말에 해당하는 영어를 빈칸에 쓰세요.

가난한	6	요리사; 요리하다	10
확인하다	7	그는 확인하고 있다	11
나무, 목재	8	그는 요리했다	12
안녕, 안녕히 가세요[계세요]	9		

Master 751~760 words

정답 p.24

⭐ 다음 각 그림과 우리말을 연결하세요. 그리고 우리말에 해당하는 영어를 빈칸에 반복해서 써보세요.

	둥근	1
	여행; 관광	2
	수프	3
	커플, 부부	4

⭐ 다음 각 우리말에 해당하는 영어를 빈칸에 쓰세요.

자랑스러운	5	긴장한	9
(맛이) 신	6	시골; 나라	10
~을 만지다	7	그는 만진다	11
~할 수 있었다	8	그는 만졌다	12

Master 761~770 words

정답 p.24

⭐ 다음 각 그림과 우리말을 연결하세요. 그리고 우리말에 해당하는 영어를 빈칸에 반복해서 써보세요.

녹음하다, 녹화하다	1
젖은	2
(기차) 선로; 경주로, 트랙	3
상자, 통	4

⭐ 다음 각 우리말에 해당하는 영어를 빈칸에 쓰세요.

잘못, 실수	5		보도하다	9
일하다	6		삼촌, 외삼촌, 고모부, 이모부	10
아니면, 또는	7		그녀는 보도하고 있다	11
상점, 가게	8		그녀는 녹음한다	12

Master 771~780 words

정답 p.24

⭐ 다음 각 그림과 우리말을 연결하세요. 그리고 우리말에 해당하는 영어를 빈칸에 반복해서 써보세요.

아래로	1
소	2
탑	3
낮은	4

⭐ 다음 각 우리말에 해당하는 영어를 빈칸에 쓰세요.

자기 자신의	5		어떻게; 얼마나	9
보여 주다	6		군중; 대중	10
느린	7		그는 따라갔다	11
따라가다, 따라오다	8			

⭐ 다음 각 그림과 우리말을 연결하세요. 그리고 우리말에 해당하는 영어를 빈칸에 반복해서 써보세요.

	테이프	1	
	헬리콥터	2	
	숟가락, 스푼	3	
	거미	4	

⭐ 다음 각 우리말에 해당하는 영어를 빈칸에 쓰세요.

컵, 잔	5		그룹, 무리, 집단	9	
저녁 식사	6		발생하다, 일어나다	10	
불평하다	7		그것은 일어났다	11	
궁전	8		그는 불평하고 있다	12	

⭐ 다음 각 그림과 우리말을 연결하세요. 그리고 우리말에 해당하는 영어를 빈칸에 반복해서 써보세요.

	가위	1	
	안경	2	
	사막	3	
	닫다	4	

⭐ 다음 각 우리말에 해당하는 영어를 빈칸에 쓰세요.

과학자	5		(값·비용이) ~이다; 값, 비용	9	
이유	6		때때로	10	
가능한	7		그것은 (값·비용이) ~이다	11	
냄새를 맡다; 냄새가 나다	8				

Master 801~810 words

정답 p.24

⭐ 다음 각 그림과 우리말을 연결하세요. 그리고 우리말에 해당하는 영어를 빈칸에 반복해서 써보세요.

			나뭇잎	1	
			큰	2	
			물고기	3	
			현금, 돈	4	

⭐ 다음 각 우리말에 해당하는 영어를 빈칸에 쓰세요.

가게, 상점	5		신선한	9
소리치다, 소리 지르다	6		모양	10
하지만, 그러나	7		그는 소리쳤다	11
희망; 바라다	8		그녀는 바란다	12

Master 811~820 words

정답 p.24

⭐ 다음 각 그림과 우리말을 연결하세요. 그리고 우리말에 해당하는 영어를 빈칸에 반복해서 써보세요.

			막대기	1	
			돌	2	
			(발)걸음	3	
			하늘	4	

⭐ 다음 각 우리말에 해당하는 영어를 빈칸에 쓰세요.

피부	5		기쁜, 반가운	9
집중하다	6		스트레스	10
바보	7		그들은 논의하고 있다	11
논의하다, 토론하다	8			

Master 821~830 words

정답 p.24

⭐ 다음 각 그림과 우리말을 연결하세요. 그리고 우리말에 해당하는 영어를 빈칸에 반복해서 써보세요.

축하하다	1	
자르다	2	
바지	3	
호랑이	4	

⭐ 다음 각 우리말에 해당하는 영어를 빈칸에 쓰세요.

문화	5		시골 지역	9
~을 향하여	6		과거	10
아름다움, 미	7		그는 자른다	11
평평한	8		그들은 축하했다	12

Master 831~840 words

정답 p.24

⭐ 다음 각 그림과 우리말을 연결하세요. 그리고 우리말에 해당하는 영어를 빈칸에 반복해서 써보세요.

때리다, 치다	1	
얇은, 가는	2	
천	3	
목욕	4	

⭐ 다음 각 우리말에 해당하는 영어를 빈칸에 쓰세요.

소개하다	5		~보다	9
다른, 그 밖의	6		죽음	10
아무것도 (~아니다[없다])	7		그녀는 소개했다	11
1000, 천	8		그는 때렸다	12

Master 841~850 words

정답 p.24

⭐ 다음 각 그림과 우리말을 연결하세요. 그리고 우리말에 해당하는 영어를 빈칸에 반복해서 써보세요.

	단추; 버튼	1	
	오리	2	
	강아지	3	
	풀, 접착제	4	

⭐ 다음 각 우리말에 해당하는 영어를 빈칸에 쓰세요.

생산하다	5		조심하는, 주의 깊은	9
인기 있는	6		사실	10
보내다	7		그것은 생산한다	11
(직장의) 일, 업무	8			

Master 851~860 words

정답 p.25

⭐ 다음 각 그림과 우리말을 연결하세요. 그리고 우리말에 해당하는 영어를 빈칸에 반복해서 써보세요.

	바이올린	1	
	불, 화재	2	
	둘 다; 양쪽의	3	
	카메라	4	

⭐ 다음 각 우리말에 해당하는 영어를 빈칸에 쓰세요.

강	5		만약 ~라면	9
언덕	6		떠나다, 출발하다	10
구하다; 저축하다	7		그는 구한다	11
정도; 수준	8		그것은 떠났다	12

Master 861~870 words

정답 p.25

⭐ 다음 각 그림과 우리말을 연결하세요. 그리고 우리말에 해당하는 영어를 빈칸에 반복해서 써보세요.

		신문	1
		두 번	2
		쓰다	3
		힘	4

⭐ 다음 각 우리말에 해당하는 영어를 빈칸에 쓰세요.

아내, 부인	5		(소)도시	9
그림	6		걱정하는	10
잠에서 깨다, 일어나다	7		그는 잠에서 깼다	11
넓은, 폭이 넓은	8			

Master 871~880 words

정답 p.25

⭐ 다음 각 그림과 우리말을 연결하세요. 그리고 우리말에 해당하는 영어를 빈칸에 반복해서 써보세요.

		경찰	1
		궁금하다	2
		샤워(하기)	3
		벤치	4

⭐ 다음 각 우리말에 해당하는 영어를 빈칸에 쓰세요.

노동자, 근로자	5		어느, 어떤	9
돼지	6		영웅	10
놓다, 두다	7		그녀는 궁금했다	11
용돈	8		그녀는 놓았다	12

⭐ 다음 각 그림과 우리말을 연결하세요. 그리고 우리말에 해당하는 영어를 빈칸에 반복해서 써보세요.

인쇄하다, 프린트하다	1	
여우	2	
사자	3	
택시	4	
중앙, 가운데	5	

⭐ 다음 각 우리말에 해당하는 영어를 빈칸에 쓰세요.

경험	6	예, 보기	9
교과서	7	신이 난, 흥분한	10
표현하다	8	그녀는 인쇄하고 있다	11

Master 891~900 words

⭐ 다음 각 그림과 우리말을 연결하세요. 그리고 우리말에 해당하는 영어를 빈칸에 반복해서 써보세요.

울다	1	
결혼하다	2	
(기름에) 굽다, 튀기다	3	
꿀	4	
돈	5	

⭐ 다음 각 우리말에 해당하는 영어를 빈칸에 쓰세요.

초등학교의	6	천천히	10
유형, 종류	7	그녀는 (기름에) 튀기고 있다	11
역사	8	그는 울고 있다	12
순환	9		

Master 901~910 words

정답 p.25

⭐ 다음 각 그림과 우리말을 연결하세요. 그리고 우리말에 해당하는 영어를 빈칸에 반복해서 써보세요.

●	●	얼룩말	1
●	●	퍼즐, 수수께끼	2
●	●	잼	3
●	●	동물원	4

⭐ 다음 각 우리말에 해당하는 영어를 빈칸에 쓰세요.

크기, 치수	5		돌다, 꺾다	9
기쁨, 즐거움	6		쇼핑몰	10
놀랄 만한, 굉장한	7		그것은 의미한다	11
의미하다	8			

Master 911~920 words

정답 p.25

⭐ 다음 각 그림과 우리말을 연결하세요. 그리고 우리말에 해당하는 영어를 빈칸에 반복해서 써보세요.

●	●	기타	1
●	●	빠른	2
●	●	언어	3
●	●	달리다, 뛰다	4
●	●	위로	5

⭐ 다음 각 우리말에 해당하는 영어를 빈칸에 쓰세요.

남자	6		꽤, 아주	9
추측하다	7		규칙	10
보통, 평소에는	8		그는 달리고 있다	11

Master 921~930 words

정답 p.25

⭐ 다음 각 그림과 우리말을 연결하세요. 그리고 우리말에 해당하는 영어를 빈칸에 반복해서 써보세요.

		카드	1	
		마당	2	
		토끼	3	
		표시	4	

⭐ 다음 각 우리말에 해당하는 영어를 빈칸에 쓰세요.

제공하다	5		일부; 부분	9
편안한	6		학년; 성적	10
관심, 흥미	7		그것은 제공한다	11
마른, 건조한	8			

Master 931~940 words

정답 p.25

⭐ 다음 각 그림과 우리말을 연결하세요. 그리고 우리말에 해당하는 영어를 빈칸에 반복해서 써보세요.

		상	1	
		애완동물	2	
		라디오	3	

⭐ 다음 각 우리말에 해당하는 영어를 빈칸에 쓰세요.

휴식; 쉬다	5		부드러운	9
과정	6		여자 분, 여성	10
왕자	6		그들은 쉬고 있다	11
비밀	7		그는 폈다	12
펴다, 펼치다	8			

Master 941~950 words

정답 p.25

⭐ 다음 각 그림과 우리말을 연결하세요. 그리고 우리말에 해당하는 영어를 빈칸에 반복해서 써보세요.

			소금	1
			비행기	2
			소파	3
			쥐	4

⭐ 다음 각 우리말에 해당하는 영어를 빈칸에 쓰세요.

힌트, 단서	5	더 많은	9
먹이를 주다	6	밖에, 밖으로	10
세일, 할인 판매	7	그는 먹이를 준다	11
도움이 되는	8		

Master 951~960 words

정답 p.25

⭐ 다음 각 그림과 우리말을 연결하세요. 그리고 우리말에 해당하는 영어를 빈칸에 반복해서 써보세요.

			(둘 중) 어느 하나(의)	1
			재킷	2
			팔다	3
			방향	4

⭐ 다음 각 우리말에 해당하는 영어를 빈칸에 쓰세요.

필요한	5	문장	9
결과	6	무서운	10
결정	7	그녀는 팔았다	11
조용한	8	그는 판다	12

⭐ 다음 각 그림과 우리말을 연결하세요. 그리고 우리말에 해당하는 영어를 빈칸에 반복해서 써보세요.

	● ●	표, 티켓	1
	● ●	거래, 무역	2
	● ●	아주 작은	3
	● ●	매운	4
	● ●	별	5

⭐ 다음 각 우리말에 해당하는 영어를 빈칸에 쓰세요.

준비하다	6		끔찍한	10	
~하게 하다	7		그녀는 ~하게 했다	11	
간단한	8		그들은 준비하고 있다	12	
쪽, 옆, 면	9				

Master 971~980 words

정답 p.26

⭐ 다음 각 그림과 우리말을 연결하세요. 그리고 우리말에 해당하는 영어를 빈칸에 반복해서 써보세요.

	● ●	밧줄	1
	● ●	한 번	2
	● ●	노래	3
	● ●	구멍	4

⭐ 다음 각 우리말에 해당하는 영어를 빈칸에 쓰세요.

~의 사이에(서)	5		옷, 의복	9	
잃어버리다; 지다	6		정부	10	
대부분, 대부분의; 가장	7		그녀는 잃어버렸다	11	
매운	8				

Master 981~990 words

⭐ 다음 각 그림과 우리말을 연결하세요. 그리고 우리말에 해당하는 영어를 빈칸에 반복해서 써보세요.

			거대한	1	
스케이트를 타다	2	
텐트, 천막	3	
외투, 코트	4	

⭐ 다음 각 우리말에 해당하는 영어를 빈칸에 쓰세요.

포옹	5		속상한, 마음이 상한	9
극장	6		경주	10
~까지	7		그녀는 스케이트를 탄다	11
(돈을) 쓰다; (시간을) 보내다	8		그는 썼다	12

Master 991~1001 words

⭐ 다음 각 그림과 우리말을 연결하세요. 그리고 우리말에 해당하는 영어를 빈칸에 반복해서 써보세요.

			수영장	1	
(두 개로 된) 한 쌍[켤레, 벌]	2	
햄버거	3	
국수	4	
정오, 낮 12시	5	

⭐ 다음 각 우리말에 해당하는 영어를 빈칸에 쓰세요.

농담	6		행동	10
멋진	7		파도	11
함께 쓰다, 공유하다	8		그들은 함께 쓰고 있다	12
페이지, 쪽	9			

쎄듀 초등 커리큘럼

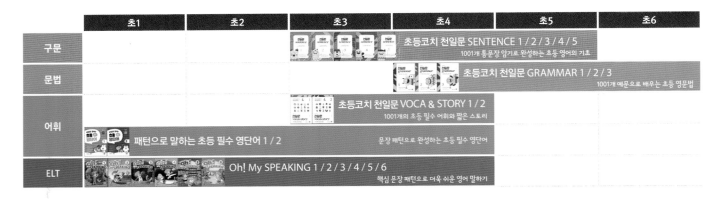

	초1	초2	초3	초4	초5	초6
구문			초등코치 천일문 SENTENCE 1 / 2 / 3 / 4 / 5			
			1001개 통문장 암기로 완성하는 초등 영어의 기초			
문법			초등코치 천일문 GRAMMAR 1 / 2 / 3			
			1001개 예문으로 배우는 초등 영문법			
어휘		초등코치 천일문 VOCA & STORY 1 / 2				
		1001개의 초등 필수 어휘와 짧은 스토리				
	패턴으로 말하는 초등 필수 영단어 1 / 2		문장 패턴으로 완성하는 초등 필수 영단어			
ELT	Oh! My SPEAKING 1 / 2 / 3 / 4 / 5 / 6			핵심 문장 패턴으로 더욱 쉬운 영어 말하기		

쎄듀 중등 커리큘럼

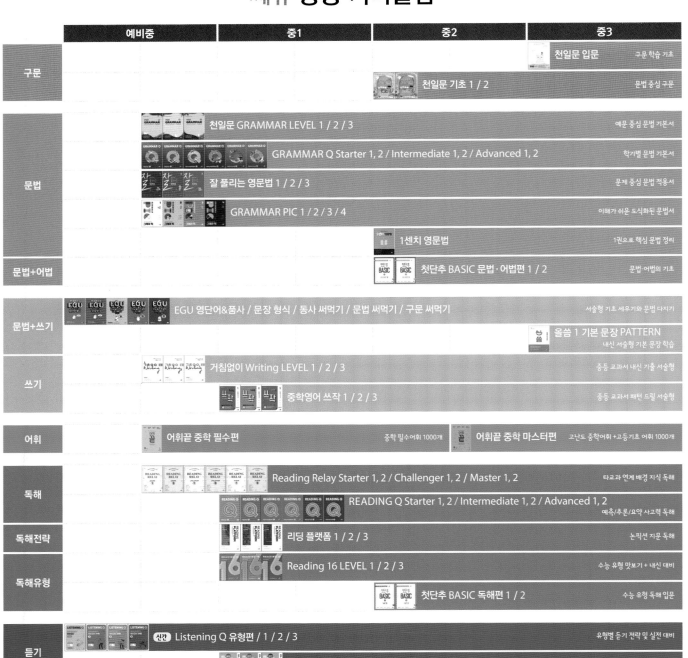

	예비중	중1	중2	중3
구문				천일문 입문 — 구문 학습 기초
		천일문 기초 1 / 2		문법 중심 구문
문법	천일문 GRAMMAR LEVEL 1 / 2 / 3			예문 중심 문법 기본서
	GRAMMAR Q Starter 1, 2 / Intermediate 1, 2 / Advanced 1, 2			학기별 문법 기본서
	잘 풀리는 영문법 1 / 2 / 3			문제 중심 문법 적용서
	GRAMMAR PIC 1 / 2 / 3 / 4			이해가 쉬운 도식화된 문법서
			1센치 영문법	1권으로 핵심 문법 정리
문법+어법		첫단추 BASIC 문법·어법편 1 / 2		문법·어법의 기초
문법+쓰기	EGU 영단어&품사 / 문장 형식 / 동사 써먹기 / 문법 써먹기 / 구문 써먹기			서술형 기초 세우기와 문법 다지기
			올쏨 1 기본 문장 PATTERN	내신 서술형 기본 문장 학습
쓰기	거침없이 Writing LEVEL 1 / 2 / 3			중등 교과서 내신 기출 서술형
	중학영어 쓰작 1 / 2 / 3			중등 교과서 패턴 드릴 서술형
어휘	어휘끝 중학 필수편		중학 필수어휘 1000개 어휘끝 중학 마스터편	고난도 중학어휘 +고등기초 어휘 1000개
독해	Reading Relay Starter 1, 2 / Challenger 1, 2 / Master 1, 2			타교과 연계 배경 지식 독해
	READING Q Starter 1, 2 / Intermediate 1, 2 / Advanced 1, 2			예측/추론/요약 사고력 독해
독해전략	리딩 플랫폼 1 / 2 / 3			논픽션 지문 독해
독해유형	Reading 16 LEVEL 1 / 2 / 3			수능 유형 맛보기 + 내신 대비
		첫단추 BASIC 독해편 1 / 2		수능 유형 독해 입문
듣기	신간 Listening Q 유형편 / 1 / 2 / 3			유형별 듣기 전략 및 실전 대비
	쎄듀 빠르게 중학영어듣기 모의고사 1 / 2 / 3			교육청 듣기평가 대비